Prodigal Daughter-Returning Home to the Father's Embrace

By

Amy Lee Kemp

Dedication

This book is dedicated to my wonderful parents, Homer Jr. and Diana. You have always supported me and held the door for me to return home. Thank you for showing me God's unconditional love and gift of no condemnation. It was through your persistent example of Christ's love that I felt it was safe to place my life in God's hands. This year marks your 42 years of marriage; I celebrate God's faithfulness in our family. Thank you for demonstrating that "nothing is impossible for those whose trust is in The Lord."

Foreword

In her book, Prodigal Daughter, Amy Lee Kemp takes you on a journey, displaying how God's amazing grace and love not only restored her life, but transformed her into the person God designed her to be from the beginning of time. It is a modern-day, real-life story of rejection, consequences, and restoration. If the story told by Jesus of the prodigal son—the son who left his family, squandered his inheritance, wound up living in poverty, yet was fully restored by his father—is meaningful to you, you will enjoy Amy's true story of her similar journey.

When we first met Amy, she was about to move to Los Angeles, California, to minister to people living in the worst of conditions—people addicted to drugs or alcohol, homeless, living in sexual immorality, and without hope. She had sold or given away almost everything she owned, including her house, automobile, and personal belongings in order to make the move from Texas to California. She went to the poor, destitute street people of Los Angeles because she had experienced that life herself and could relate to those people and their condition. She had experienced the deliverance from such conditions, as well as the full and complete restoration to her family and, more importantly, to her God.

We have had the privilege to watch Amy grow in her ministry since her response, years ago, to the work in Los Angeles. She has since ministered to the down-and-out in many cities, working with churches on a national and international level.

And now, she has finally documented her story in a manner that allows us to see, feel, and share her feelings of hopelessness and failure as well as her joy of finding herself and her salvation.

Are you on a journey of hopelessness?

Do you have a "prodigal son or daughter"?

Do you have a grandchild or other loved ones that have rejected God and are living a life of hopelessness?

If so, this book is a must-read.

Shannon and Randy Stevenson

Contents

Dedication...iii

Foreword..v

Preface...ix

Chapter 1—A Secret Pain Hidden Luke 15:11–31 1

Chapter 2—I Knew I was Different 9

Chapter 3—My Season Ended...12

Chapter 4—The Fight was Exhausting.................................15

Chapter 5—Grace would Teach Me 18

Chapter 6—Stop Frustrating My Grace!...............................21

Chapter 7— Religious Captivity 25

Chapter 8—Moving Forward 29

Chapter 9—A Choice to Make..32

Chapter 10—Jesus is the Answer.....................................35

Chapter 11—Forever a Daughter......................................38

Chapter 12—Quick, Grab the Robe...................................44

Chapter 13—Utter Dependence 46

Chapter 14—It's Safe to Let Go 51

Chapter 15—Accepted in the Beloved 57

Chapter 16—I Remember their Sins No More..........................65

Chapter 17—A Song in Heaven.......................................68

Chapter 18—Prodigal Prayer...72

Acknowledgements..73

Author Bio..77

Partner with Me Today...78

Recommended Resources...81

Preface

The people that sat in darkness saw a great light, and to them that sat in the region
and shadow of death, to them did light spring up.
(Matthew 4:16 ASV)

WE ARE CALLED to be people of the "light" and disciples of the "light." This is
the full measure and vision for this book and my service to the Kingdom. The
light of Christ impacts lives. Without the light of Christ, we can't see the hope we
have in Christ, so there is mass darkness. Many are trapped in the dark and live
in fear, judgment, hurt, sickness, and condemnation. They know no other way,
and they are longing for peace and for life. The pages of this book are filled with
my story and life lessons through pain, despair, and hopelessness. The light of
Christ was lit in my heart at the age of six, and though the darkness of substance
abuse, suicide attempts, rejection, and homosexuality clouded my view, the light
of Christ remained.

My hope is to turn on the light of Christ through my journey so that people
can walk in the light and never return to darkness. When the light of Christ's
love comes in and we are able to see, we will realize that we have value, that we
are loved, and that we are true children of God. We cannot have truth until we
can see truth. When the truth comes in the heart, the light of Christ bursts forth,
deception is exposed, and people are set free.

As I look around, I see my generation being preyed upon to endorse the bondage that Christ came to destroy. The battle is in full swing against the children of God; my hope is to reveal to the sons and daughters of God their privileges and design. Through the demonstration of the Father's love that was displayed at Calvary, we are children of God, who can boldly declare a spiritual identity as the righteousness of God in Christ.

I've thrown myself headlong into your arms - I'm celebrating your rescue. Psalm 13:5 MSG

CHAPTER 1

A Secret Pain Hidden
Luke 15:11–31

THE YOUNG BOY approached his father, "I don't want to wait any longer. I want my portion of the inheritance!" The father stared into his son's eyes in complete shock, questioning in his heart why his son was so upset. His son's countenance had changed, his eyes were pierced with firmness, his hands gripped tightly upon his hips, and his head was held high; he was not going to budge until his father gave him what he wanted. With love in his eyes, the father said, "Okay, son, I will give you your portion of the inheritance."

A few days later, the young boy packed all of his belongings and took a trip into the city where he would experience the real life—city life. Everything he had ever desired to enjoy was now his, and nothing could stop him from experiencing the high life he had always dreamed about. His money went quickly. Soon, the young boy found himself with no money, no home, and all his night-life friends had disappeared; he was left all alone. He went many days wandering throughout the city—tired, dirty, lonely, and hungry.

One day, the young boy met a farmer and persuaded the farmer to hire him. The only job the farmer had was feeding his pigs. The boy thought, "At least, I'll have a place to lay my head," so he agreed to work for the farmer. The farmer didn't give the young boy anything to eat; day after day, he fed the pigs and went without. The boy was starving. He looked at the pigs food one afternoon and thought out loud, "That looks good." As those words came from his lips, shame gripped his heart. He wiped the tears from his eyes and sat down. He thought, "How did I get here! I want to go home to my father."

The boy realized that even his father's hired hands had food to eat. He thought, "I know what I'll do; I'll return to my father, ask for his forgiveness, and perhaps he will hire me to be one of his hired hands." As the boy started home, he began rehearsing his speech to his father. "I know I have sinned against both you and God, and I'm no longer worthy to be called your son. Please, father, make me your hired hand."

The young boy was a distance from his home when his father spotted him on the horizon; tears filled the father's eyes as he ran across the field toward his son. When the father reached the boy, he grabbed him, kissed him, and rejoiced with loud cries of joy, "Oh, how I've missed you son. My boy has come home!" The boy was overwhelmed with emotion by his father's welcome. The father yelled, "Servants, quick go get the finest robe from the house and put it on my son, get a ring for his finger, and sandals for his feet. And go get the calf we have been fattening, for my beloved son is home; it is time to rejoice. Prepare for a celebration tonight in my son's honor (Luke 15:11–24 Paraphrased). The young boy in the story was me.

As far back as I can remember, I felt insecure and different from other girls. I grew up with two sisters; I was in the middle. Both of my sisters were extremely girly. They loved all the typical things little girls liked: dolls, fluffy dresses, and playing dress-up with mom's make-up and high heels. I was just the opposite. I despised anything that appeared girly. I hated to wear dresses, especially pink dresses, and the thought of playing with Barbie dolls made me angry. I felt safe and content, playing with a G. I. Joe, action figures, cars, play-guns, and transformers.

Growing up with two sisters and seven girl cousins left me playing alone much of the time; there were a few exceptions when my cousins would talk me into playing dolls. I agreed to play along only if I could be the car that drove the families around. I was pretty good at hiding my feelings of anger and rejection on the outside as I hid behind a smirky smile. But I knew what was behind it—**a secret hidden pain.**

As a pastor's daughter, I grew up in a strong, Christian family. When I was six, my dad decided to resign from his church. My parents wanted to move back to Dallas, Texas, to be close to my grandparents who were pastors of a small non-denominational church. I accepted Jesus into my heart when I was six and was baptized when I was seven. I loved Jesus, and I knew all the Bible stories, like David and Goliath, Sampson and Delilah, and the three Hebrew boys. Being in church three times during a week was pretty normal for my family.

My family was very religious. I grew up hearing about God's love, but strife and division within my family silenced God's love in my heart. My family and I attended my grandparent's church. Outwardly, the church appeared to be very spiritual, but there was a lot of verbal abuse, along with some physical abuse. I can remember one incident when the service was extremely emotional, and I hid underneath the pew in fear. Due to the misuse of the spirit by individuals wanting to control others, my view of God became distorted.

Then, when I was eight-years-old, my parents started having problems in their marriage. One day after school, my dad decided to leave my mom, my two sisters, and me. I resented him for abandoning me. In order to protect us, my mom kept the conflict hidden from my sisters and me. My dad was away for a few months but, eventually, came back home to work things out with my mom.

The summer before I started fourth grade, I began experimenting with alcohol and cigarettes, along with some older kids who lived down the street from my house. I had a great need to feel accepted by my friends. When I hung out with the older kids, it helped me block out the feelings of loneliness. I felt acceptance where I had previously felt rejection. When I began Junior High school (13-years-old), things seemed to get better for me. I began to find my acceptance with the game of basketball. It was quite obvious that I had been gifted with a natural ability to play the game. During my seventh- and eighth-grade year, I became "the" girl athlete in the school, scoring as high as 40 points a game. Basketball became my life. My whole identity was wrapped up in basketball. I can remember watching women's basketball on television and dreaming of become a college superstar.

Later that year, I began going to parties, drinking, and flirting with sexual temptations. I wanted to fit in with all the other girls but felt I was perceived differently because of my athletic prowess. Some considered me to be a tomboy. I had a few boyfriends but nothing ever serious. I was truly empty inside.

As my eighth-grade year progressed, I became increasingly depressed. The conditions at home were uncertain, and the thought of my parents separating again was too much. I couldn't carry the weight of the rejection I felt, so I just snapped. I was so tired of feeling empty, so I decided to end my life. I picked up the phone, called my best friend, and told her goodbye. I asked her to tell my basketball coach goodbye and, then, hung up the phone. I locked myself in the bathroom and downed a bottle of aspirin; the count was 500. I thought to myself, "If I can just fall asleep, things will go away, and I won't feel empty anymore." But to my surprise, my mom found me and rushed me to the hospital. The doctors pumped my stomach, and my life was spared.

That very day my parents separated. While lying in my hospital bed, my mom walked over to me and began to tell me that a woman was going to come in to question me. She told me if I appeared to be a risk to myself, I would be placed in a special hospital. My mom looked at me with eyes of desperation. I quickly stuffed my brokenness down and sat up in the bed and said, "Okay, I will tell her I am all right." Fear gripped my heart because I didn't want to be sent away from my mom. I remember telling myself to get it together and to be strong.

Hours later, the woman came in and questioned me. I told her that I was okay and didn't want to die; I just wanted my parent's attention. Deep down, I knew that wasn't true because at the time, I didn't want to live. I felt hopeless and broken beyond repair. At that point, I knew I couldn't lay my brokenness on my parent's shoulders; I was going to have to carry my own pain. The attempts to mask my pain with an outward show only left me to feel more isolated. The next morning, I left the hospital, and my suicide attempt was never mentioned again. My hidden pain of abandonment began to take form, and I began to show my anger externally. I began picking fights at school, and I stayed away from home as much as possible.

During the summer prior to my ninth-grade year (15-years-old), God began restoring my parents' marriage. This time, my dad returned to place his life and their marriage back in the hands of God. My parents decided to start over and get away from the city and the noise. So we moved to a small town in East Texas. The decision my parents made was in our family's best interest, but my sisters and I faced leaving all our friends and comfort. This move was very hard for me because I didn't know anyone in the town, and the thought of not being accepted was overwhelming. Starting school was desperately hard for me because I had no idea how to fit in or what to expect. Within the first semester of school, my athletic abilities proved to pay off. I was chosen to play varsity basketball as a freshman. Hanging out with the older crowd began to really influence my decisions, and I quickly found myself going to nightclubs, drinking, and partying.

During my sophomore year (16-years-old), I was introduced to a lifestyle of homosexuality. My surroundings quickly pressed heavy upon my thoughts, and I began questioning my identity, and my femininity. My thoughts about boys were so different from most girls—I didn't trust boys. Most of the boys I knew pretended to like you but, then, would press you to get physical. I did not understand why boys couldn't just like me without a selfishness attached. I wanted to be loved for me. I wanted to be accepted and chosen for me. My questionings kept me isolated and lost.

Then, in my eleventh-grade year of high school, I was kicked out of school for fighting. The anger and emptiness inside numbed my feelings. The following year, I found myself behind bars after a long weekend of partying and fighting. Being arrested and spending time in jail didn't scare me because I knew I could call a friend, who would come, pay the fine, and bail me out. I believe the bitterness and anger in my heart toward my parents and myself pushed me to believe a lie. I didn't think I had any value. I thought God made a mistake.

As I continued in my rebellious lifestyle, everything about me changed. I became more involved with drugs, and I ran away from anyone who wanted to tell me about God's love. Furthermore, the pain in my heart pushed me to believe I was invincible. At the time, I may have appeared to be strong on the outside, but inside I was totally broken; however, I really just wanted to be loved and accepted. I felt I was held captive with no way of escape, and I was afraid.

By my senior year of high school, things were out of control, a serious relationship I was in ended. I became very depressed and dropped out of school. At this point in my life, everything was stripped from me—my purity, education, future of playing college basketball, and family. After a disagreement with my mom about my lifestyle, I decided to move out of my parents' home. And for the next five years, I ran from everyone and everything that I had previously held valuable.

So I left my parents' home with all my belongings and spent the night at my best friend's house. I was now free to do whatever I wanted, and no one could stop me from experiencing the life I had always dreamed of having. The next morning, a guy friend, who was a local drug dealer, invited me to move in with him and his brother. My friend was like a brother; he took good care of me and made sure I had money for food and all the entertainment I could enjoy. Living in that environment began to take a toll on me; I didn't like all the new faces of men who came by daily

After that, I decided to pack a few clothes and take off with two friends to the city of Dallas. I didn't know my two friends very well, but I thought anything could be better than the environment in which I was living. My two friends and I spent every night at the dance club. In the past, I had gone to local, small-town clubs but had never experienced the nightlife in the city. My first impression of the city life was exciting; I had never seen such a large community of gay pride. The city life was fast; it was just a big party where anything goes. I embraced the city life and spent every night at the club. However, my friends and I didn't have an apartment of our own or a job.

The first weekend we arrived in Dallas, my (male) friend decided that one of us needed to get hooked up so we could have a place to stay. I remember feeling so dirty at his comment and refused in my heart. At the end of the night, he walked over to me and said, "Amy, meet this person and act interested, so we can have a place to stay." I walked away from him and told him to hook up with her himself. After we ate and sobered up at a local Denny's, we drove the two hours back to my hometown. The next night, we drove back into the city. That night my (male) friend met another man and we stayed at his home. I slept during the day and partied all night, until 4 a.m. in the morning. My (male) friend would steal items and get cash back to fund our party life. Our increasing cash flow allowed me to take a lot of speed, mixed with alcohol.

I remember one particular night after the bar closed when I jumped in a new friend's convertible and drove back to my friend's place. We were both drunk; neither one of us could stand up, much less drive. In the pouring down rain, top down, we drove 120 mph down the middle of the highway. On another night, I was pulled over by a police officer for swerving from lane to lane. As I stood at the back of the car, I knew if I didn't get my act together, I was going to jail. The officer had me stand on one leg and touch my nose with the tip of my finger. It was the grace of God that I didn't go to jail on that night or die in a car accident. If the officer had administered a Breathalyzer test to me, I would have been arrested.

After a while, it seemed my days ran together. I went from relationship to relationship. And no matter how much drugs, alcohol, or physical pleasure with which I became involved, it never dulled the pain nor satisfied the longing for love in my heart

In 1998, after a long night of partying with friends and being high for several days, I came to a crossroad. I remember sitting alone, curled up in a fetal position, scared, and thinking that the drug I was doing was going to swallow me up. In complete shame, I thought, "How did I end up here? How do I get out of this mess?" As I sat there alone on the couch, staring at the wall, the song I had learned as a kid began swelling up inside me, and I began to sing, "Jesus loves me this I know, for the Bible tells me so." I started crying very hard. I asked God that if He would let me come off drugs that I would commit my life to him. As I was saying those words, my heart began to feel peace and, shortly after, I fell asleep.

In our darkest moments, we are never alone. Have you ever made poor decisions and felt that shame had covered your nakedness? You are not alone; Father God sees you, and your mistakes have not scared Him away. He says, "For I hold you by your right hand—I, the Lord your God. And I say to you, 'Do not be afraid. I am here to help you" (Isaiah 41:13 NLT). His hand is placed in yours; grip His hand and receive his help.

On the next day, a friend came by to party and hang out. I asked her if she could run me by my parents' house. At that point, I hadn't had anything to do with my parents for five years. My parents didn't agree with my lifestyle choices, and when I was around them, I felt convicted, so I just stayed away. When I walked in, I just collapsed, crying and saying, "I'm tired, I'm so tired mom." At that very moment, my mom and dad began praying over me. As tears filled the floor, my mom asked me if I wanted to pray and ask God to forgive me. I said, "Yes, mom! Yes, I'm so tired!" I prayed and asked God to forgive me for my sins and to help me change. I knew in my heart that He was the only one that could take all the hurt, shame, and disappointment from me and give me peace. And, oh how, I needed peace!

God had previously knocked many times at my heart, but the hurt and decisions I had made caused me to feel hopeless. I had made so many mistakes that I didn't know where to begin, and the thought of admitting I was wrong about God and my lifestyle, was too painful. If it hadn't been for God's persistent **love** pursuing me, I don't think I would be alive to share my story.

Friends, we all have gone astray from home at some point. It doesn't matter how far you have traveled, you are always welcome to return home. The Father is standing on the horizon, looking and waiting to embrace you, to dress you in the finest robe, to place the ring on your finger and sandals on your feet. Come on; let's start the journey toward home.

CHAPTER 2

I Knew I was Different

THE DAY I walked into my parents' home was the last day I embraced my past. I cut all ties to friends. I quit my job because I worked with friends with whom I partied, and I refused all phone calls from everyone. I knew in my heart that I couldn't look back. The only way I was going to heal was to find out who God says I am in Christ.

I was given a book by Joyce Meyer called *Battlefield of the Mind*. While reading the book, the Lord helped me see the label of homosexuality that I had placed on myself was not true. Little by little, He began to peel back the lies that were rooted in the feelings of abandonment. The opposite of truth is deception. When we accept a thought that's contrary to the Word of God, we make an agreement with Satan. An agreement with an evil thought gives Satan authority to build a stronghold in our mind. My anger and distrust in men caused me to live in bondage. I saw myself as a failure and, therefore, rejected my femininity. I hid behind baseball caps, baggy jeans, and polo shirts. My attempt wasn't to be a man, but I desired deep within my heart to create my own family. I wanted someone to care for, and I wanted someone to care for me. I thought if I took control, I could experience a perfect family. I believed the lie that I could undo my own pain by taking the role of a husband. I believed the feelings of abandonment would stop if I gave to someone what I always needed from my dad, but just the opposite happened. The more I tried to give love, the emptier I felt. Emptiness left me feeling hopeless, worn out, used up, exhausted, and alone.

Do you feel empty inside? Feeling inner emptiness comes from a false belief. Many times, we try to feed our inner emptiness with food, alcohol, drugs, activities, (business) work, shopping, sports, or with a relationship. Our emptiness may be satisfied for a short time, but, soon, the emptiness is back, and we begin looking for another substance to fill up the gaping hole in our hearts. Only God can fill the emptiness of our souls. Jesus said, " . . . If any man is thirsty, let him come to Me and drink! He who believes in Me [who cleaves to and trusts in and relies on Me] as the Scripture has said, From his innermost being shall flow [continually] springs and rivers of living water" (John 7:37–38 AMP).

After my sinner's prayer, I knew I was different. The feelings I once felt of rejection, shame, guilt, and loneliness were gone. In Romans 5:5, Paul tells us that the love of God is poured into our hearts by the Holy Spirit. The fullness of God Himself comes into our heart and takes up permanent residence in us. Where I was once spiritually dead to God, I was now alive and overflowing with God, filled with His nature, His life, and ruled by Him: "For of His fullness have we all received, and grace upon grace" (John 1:16 ASV). That means I had now received His love life. No longer would I be dominated and ruled by my feelings, thoughts of condemnation, and my past mistakes. I was free to embrace the love nature of God and live in the realm of His love for me: "... who delivered us out of the power of darkness, and translated us into the kingdom of the Son of His love" (Colossians 1:13 ASV). This is one of my favorite verses in the entire Bible. God translated me out of rejection, anger, and fear and placed me in His love. My feelings of abandonment were swallowed up by love.

As I began to read the Bible, I discovered God's passionate love for me. He said . . .

Before I created the world, I loved you. I chose you in Christ to be holy and I see you without fault in my eyes. My unchanging plan has always been to adopt you into My family by bringing you to Myself through My Son Jesus. And this gave me great pleasure. I purchased your freedom through the blood of My Son, and your sins I have forgiven. I shower you with my kindness. I have poured my wisdom and understanding on you. My purpose is that you will trust in Christ and believe I have identified you as my own child. I have given the Holy Spirit as My guarantee to you that I gave you a glorious inheritance in Christ. (Ephesians 1:3–12 Paraphrased)

God had adopted me into His family when I was six-years-old. He chose me and took the responsibility to be my Father. But because I didn't understand how much Father God loved me, I felt utterly hopeless and rejected.

I wandered away from home in rebellion, thinking I would find fulfillment, love, and acceptance—myself. But like the prodigal son, I, too, quickly found that the fleeting pleasures of sin would leave me hurt, ashamed, disappointed, and feeling unworthy. The writer of Hebrews wrote that 'sin is pleasurable for a season" (11:25 Paraphrased). With loving compassion, God was standing on the horizon patiently waiting for me to head home. The moment I started toward home, by calling out to Him for help, He came running with all the forces of Heaven and snatched me up out of Satan's hands:

I rescue my sheep from the enemy's mouth; the sheep will no longer be their prey. For I the Sovereign Lord, search and find my lost sheep. I rescue them. I bring them back home. I myself tend to them and cause them to lie down in peace. I search for my lost ones who strayed away, and I bring them safely home again. I bind up the injured and strengthen the weak. (Ezekiel 34:10 NLT)

You, reader, may be asking, "Why would God want to rescue me? I've made too many mistakes, and I do not have any strength left!" Friends, God comes to our rescue because He loves us. It doesn't matter how many mistakes you've made in life, His shoulders are strong enough to carry you. Don't run; surrender to His care and drink freely. He will shower your heart with love, quench your thirst, and give your soul rest.

CHAPTER 3

My Season Ended

THERE WAS NO longer pleasure in drugs, alcohol, sex, and violence. The pleasure that sin once brought began to suck me down into a whirlwind. The devil's plan is three-fold: **to steal, to kill and to destroy**. First Peter 5:8 states, "Stay alert! Watch out for your great enemy, the devil. He prowls around like a roaring lion, looking for someone to devour (NLT)." The devil has no plan for us except to steal, kill, and destroy. Jesus said that the devil comes ONLY...." This means that surely the devil will come, but when he comes he has no other interest or purpose for us but ONLY one thing. He comes to kill us with condemnation when we fail. But Jesus comes to give us life! "[It is He] Who has qualified us [making us to be fit and worthy and sufficient] as ministers and dispensers of a new covenant [of salvation through Christ], no [ministers] of the letter of (of legally written code) but of the Spirit; for the code [of the law] kills, but the [Holy] Spirit makes alive" (2 Corinthians 3:6 AMP.

When we take the devil's bait of condemnation and believe the lie that God is angry with us when we fail, we begin to feel unworthy. The feeling of unworthiness opens the door for Satan to steal from us. He comes to steal our identity. We are children of God, but if Satan can make us think that our sinful behavior separates us from God, we'll turn over our authority to him and give him open access to destroy us:

> [It is He] Who has qualified us [making us to be fit and worthy and sufficient] as ministers and dispensers of a new covenant [of salvation through Christ], no [ministers] of the letter of (of legally written code) but of the Spirit; for the code [of the law] kills, but the [Holy] Spirit makes alive. (Romans 8:1–4 NLT)

Jesus was teaching at the temple when the Pharisees and the teachers of religious law brought a woman, who was caught red-handed in the act of adultery, before Him. The men threw the woman in the midst of the crowd. The men had no interest in her; neither did they have any compassion. They had only one goal, which was to trap Jesus into saying something they could use against him. A large crowd gathered, mocking and laughing, as the woman stood there barely clothed. Jesus looked at the woman and saw her pain. He saw her shame.

With love in His eyes, Jesus knew that the Father's love and forgiveness would heal the woman's brokenness: "'Teacher,' they said to Jesus, 'this woman was caught in the act of adultery. The law of Moses says to stone her. What do you say?' ... but Jesus stooped down and wrote in the dust with his finger.... 'All right, but let the one who has never sinned throw the first stone'" (John 8:4–8 NLT). The scribes and Pharisees began to leave, one by one, till none of them were left. Those who wanted to condemn the woman could not. But Jesus, the only one in the crowd who had the power to condemn her, would not. "Then Jesus stood up again and said to the woman, 'Where are your accusers? Didn't even one of them condemn you'" (v. 9 NLT)? For the first time, the woman was not met with judgment but with grace. She looked up toward Him in shame and answered Jesus, "'No one condemns me, Lord.' Jesus said, 'Neither do I condemn you; go and sin no more'" (vv. 10–11 Paraphrased). All of her life she had never encountered such love. Love that looked past her sins, saw her pain, and gave forgiveness so freely. Her heart was captivated! When she received the gift of no condemnation, it gave her the power to " ... go and sin no more" (v. 11 NLT).

Satan's devious and deceitful nature is identified as "father of lies" (John 8:44 NLT). He disguises himself as an angel of light in order to deceive all of mankind into thinking God is angry with us when we sin. His tactic is to disqualify us. Satan comes with condemnation (fear, guilt). Unfortunately, people, who do not understand God's grace, jump on the bandwagon in judgment, but the book of Titus writes, "For the grace of God (His unmerited favor and blessing) has come forward (appeared) for the deliverance from sin and the eternal salvation for all mankind.

It has trained us to reject and renounce all ungodliness (irreligion) and worldly (passionate) desires, to live discreet (temperate, self-controlled), upright, devout (spiritually whole) lives in this present world..." (Titus 2: 11–12 AMP)

Natural laws of nature reveal God's grace. For we know that's it's impossible to clean a fish before you catch it. Likewise, unless we receive the gift of no condemnation, we will be powerless to overcome the struggles in the flesh.

CHAPTER 4

The Fight was Exhausting

In 1999, the opportunity and dream I thought was lost forever was restored. A friend from church sent a recommendation to a local college. I was invited to come and tryout to play basketball for Southwestern Assembly of God University. I went for the tryout and was invited to come and play basketball. While I was attending Bible College, God began speaking to my heart to share with others what I've been through and to tell them about the grace of God that's big enough to save them from the deepest pit and restore their mind, relationships, and future.

At that time in my life, I developed a deep, love for God so much and wanted to learn more about the Bible. So I began asking a friend's dad some questions; he was a pastor of a church. He told me that if I sinned, then, God would leave me—that I would lose my salvation. I didn't know how to be perfect. Those words left me feeling guilty and condemned. I did not want to disappoint or let God down after all He had done for me. Once again, the feelings of insecurity began to take over my thoughts, leaving me to feel all alone and worthless. I tried with all my might to be obedient to God's Word. I confessed every sin I could think of that I might have committed because I didn't want God to leave me. I became more conscious of my sinful behavior than of God's loving grace.

Before the first year of Bible College was over, I was approached by a girl who wanted to befriend me. She had attended the school for the past three years and offered to show me around campus. Within a few weeks, I compromised and went into the city to meet up with friends at a bar. That one night turned into three months, and I, eventually, walked away from school. I felt guilty about my actions, and I didn't know how to turn things around. The best thing I knew to do was to return home to my parents where it was safe, and that's just what I did. I returned home with my head down in shame. I hid my feelings, once again, behind that familiar, smirky smile. I blamed my coach's attitude as my reason for leaving school. Once again, I found myself feeling abandoned. That time, it wasn't my parents, but it was God who abandoned me.

During that year, I worked really hard to be good. I attended church, I read my Bible, and I listened to only Christian music. It seemed my life began to take form again. At the end of that year, I moved to the city to meet up with a friend from school who was a musician. I got a job at a local Christian bookstore, managing the children's department, and I attended a good church. Outwardly, I appeared to be a strong Christian girl, but, inside, I was jealous, insecure, and guilty feelings dominated my thoughts. I renewed my mind, daily, to God's Word, but it seemed my struggles grew. There would be days that I spent more time casting down thoughts than enjoying a normal thought. The fight was exhausting! I had a strong will and determination not to give in to the temptations of the flesh, but to be honest, I failed at every attempt. The more I tried not to be jealous or envious, the more I felt jealous and envious: The Word says …

> Do not be conformed to this world (this age), [fashioned after and adapted to its external, superficial customs], but be transformed (changed) by the [entire] renewal of your mind [by its new ideals and its new attitude], so that you may prove [for yourselves] what is the good and acceptable and perfect will of God, even the thing which is good and acceptable and perfect will of God, even the thing which is good and acceptable and perfect [in His sight for you (Romans 12:2 AMP).

I would tell myself, I had the power to change. God has not given us a spirit of fear, but He has given us a spirit of power, a well-balanced mind and self-discipline (2 Timothy 1:7 NLT). I took this scripture by the hand and laid claim that I would get results if I kept confessing the Word and casting down wrong thoughts. The problem with my idea was that I wasn't leaning upon the power of the Holy Spirit to change me. I took the responsibility into my *own* hands;

I thought that by sheer willpower, I would be able to defeat sinful thoughts and behavior.

How do you combat thoughts? Are you in a combat with negative thoughts right now? Do you feel drained of energy? When you find yourself thinking something bad, stop and ask God to help you. He will immediately respond, confirming that the negative thought was not from him. The combat is impossible to win in your mind without replacing the negative thought with God's word. Satan launches arrows (negative thoughts) towards us to get us sidetracked into self-examination. If Satan can get you fixed on trying to fight unwanted thoughts with another thought instead of the Word, he will convince you when you fail that God is repulsed. Satan wants you to push God away. Instead of knowing how loving, powerful, and faithful God really is, you will render Him defenseless. The truth is, the moment a negative thought is held up against the blood of Christ, the negative thought will tap out in defeat. The next time a negative thought comes, run to the battlefront declaring, "God loves me," and watch the thought scatter in fear.

CHAPTER 5

Grace would Teach Me

I HAD NEVER played any instrument, but the desire to play drums flourished in my heart. The first time I sat down at the drums to jam with a friend, I was amazed I could hear and play along with the rhythm. The Lord really blessed my desire for drums, and I quickly learned to play and joined my friend in her band. Soon, we began to travel around the United States, telling others about God's forgiveness and freedom from homosexuality. During this time, my thoughts of not being good enough really influenced my perception of how others saw me. I supported my band but never had the courage to share my story. When God intervened in my life, rescuing me from drugs, homosexuality, suicidal thoughts, and depression, He became my superhero—my knight in shining armor. But now, my image of God was one who sat on his throne judging and being angry with me when I sinned.

In 2002, after a downward spiral of compromise in my band, I decided to walk away from my band and God. I remember telling God that I loved him, but I was mad at Him about how things turned out. I made a declaration that I wouldn't go back to drugs, alcohol, or nightclubs, but I was not going to serve or talk with him any longer. For the next two years, I wandered around trying to figure out where I fit. Within a matter of months, I found myself compromising and back in the pit of lies and accepting the label of my past. I was extremely lonely during this time in my life, and I didn't have anyone to talk with that I could trust. I judged myself guilty. I thought if God is judging me every time I have a sinful thought or action, then there's no hope for me to change.

Even though I put my fist up in God's face, He kept on loving me. In 2004, I woke up one morning, grabbed my Bible, and sat at the kitchen table. I told God how lonely I was and that I knew I rejected him. I also told Him that I was sorry. My worst day with God was better than my best day running from Him. That morning, I wrote in the front of my Bible, "Today, September 7, 2004, I choose to trust You. I want to walk with You, God." I found myself standing inside the pig's pen, broken, lonely, and missing home. All I wanted was to go home to my daddy.

I wanted to be reconciled with God. I wanted to follow Him and live for Him. I wanted to leave the past behind. I reached out to God for love and forgiveness, and He freely extended grace. I thought I was walking toward God, but He was walking with me the whole time:

I will never leave nor forsake you. (Hebrews 13:5 NLT)
I'm the friend that sticks closer than a brother. (Proverbs 18:24 NLT)

Trusting God can be tiresome, but it doesn't have to be. When we release control, stop being hard with ourselves, and stop trying to change things in our own strength, we'll experience the power of God's grace, which has defeated our struggles. We begin with not looking back with regret. Regret's aim is to heap condemnation, guilt, and fear into our hearts to prevent us from moving forward:

Brethren I count not myself to have apprehended: but this one thing I do, forgetting those things which are behind, and reaching forth unto those things which are before, I press toward the mark for the prize of the high calling of God in Christ Jesus. (Philippians 3:13–14 AMP) Even though your situation may look hopeless, once it's placed in God's hands, He will make good from it. Don't doubt. God's hands are big:

I give them eternal life, and they will never perish. No one can snatch them away from me, for my Father, who has given them to me, and he is more powerful than anyone. No one is able to snatch them out. Of the Father's hand. The Father and I are one. (John 10:28–30 NLT)

When we believe in our hearts and confess Jesus is the Son of God, we receive eternal life. Eternal life is the gift of spending eternity with God in heaven, never to taste death because Christ has accomplished it for us. It's also the gift of fellowship with the Father on earth. Life is the gift of enjoying the God-kind of life. This gift of life isn't a gift for us to enjoy when we go to heaven, but it's one in which the Father has given for us to enjoy now. The conditions of my lifestyle didn't change, immediately, but there was a change inside my heart. The rebellion in my heart toward God was exchanged for love. I didn't know how to change the outward conditions of my choices, but I no longer had a desire for the things I once enjoyed. The battle was over in my heart; I just didn't know how to move forward, but grace would teach me.

CHAPTER 6

Stop Frustrating My Grace!

I DECIDED TO give church another chance. I started attending church on a regular basis and watched a great deal of Christian television. The message I was hearing was I must do, obey, and earn in order for God to bless and extend grace to me. I was so confused. This message and my personal experience of God's grace in my life didn't match up. I couldn't figure out what or who was correct.

One night while watching a Christian television program I asked God, "What is grace?" I hear a lot about it; I think I've experienced it, but I need to know what it is and if I'm supposed to live by it. Jesus came to reveal the nature of the Father to us: "If you had really known me, you would know who my Father is.... Anyone who has seen Me has seen the Father (John 14:7, 9 NLT). Jesus came to reveal the Father and to offer a relationship with Him. Jesus and the Father is not the same person, but they are of the same nature and character (two persons of the triune Godhead). The way Jesus interacted with people and the compassion he displayed was exactly how the Father felt.

The message of the gospel of grace is twofold:

1. Jesus died for us (took all our sins, sickness, poverty, shame).

2. Jesus died as us (including us in his death, burial, and resurrection to kill the old man and resurrect us into new life with a new heart and a new spirit).

This was not His only assignment. He came to reveal the Father and to change the way we see God. He came with a mission to reveal the Father and destroy the works of the devil in our behalf at the cross. Once our sin debt is paid, we gain access to the throne of God to receive His mercy and find grace in the time of need. No longer are we slaves of sin, but, now, we are children of God.

The tragedy is that many Christians today have a distant unapproachable God. They live a "disconnected" form of Christianity—distant and filled with a form of religion and ritual but lacking the profound interaction of intimacy with God's heart that is available to them every day. Jesus sent us the Holy Spirit to reveal the tender, compassionate, and loving Father, who desires intimacy with us—an intimacy one can approach with reverent confidence:

Let us go right into the presence of God with sincere hearts fully trusting him. For our guilty consciences have been sprinkled with Christ's blood to make us clean, and our bodies have been washed with pure water. Let us hold tightly without wavering to the hope we affirm, for God can be trusted to keep his promise. (Hebrews 10:22–23 NLT)

Over the next year, God began introducing me to grace. He showed me that grace is a person. Grace is Jesus. One afternoon while thinking about what I've been through in my life, God spoke very directly to my heart. He told me, "Amy, it's going to be hard. It will be painful, but I will never ever leave you." I remember having so much peace in my heart, and I said, "Okay, God." Slowly, God began to point out all the lies I've believed about His character. He showed me through His Word how His Son, Jesus, had borne all my sins, took my punishment for sin, and bore His anger against me:

For you were buried with Christ when you were baptized. And with him you were raised to a new life because you trusted the mighty power of God, who raised Christ from the dead. You were dead because of your sins and because your sinful nature was not yet cut away. Then God made you alive with Christ, for he forgave all your sins. He canceled the record of the charges against us and took it away by nailing it to cross. In this way, God disarmed the spiritual rulers and authorities. He shamed them publicly by his victory over them on the cross." (Colossians 2:12–15 NLT)

I wanted to trust God and understand His grace, but to be honest; it was most difficult for me. I'll never forget one day when God spoke to my heart through a passage of Scripture: (Galatians 2:21 Paraphrased). He said, "Stop frustrating my grace!" In total shock, I thought to myself, "What does that mean?" God was trying to show me that as long as I thought I had to earn his love, I could never receive it freely. The law *demands* from us, but grace *gives*. The demand I placed myself under made me aware of my sin, and I felt guilty all the time. When we try to make ourselves right with God by rule keeping, Christ becomes of no effect to us. We are cut off from Christ and fall from God's grace:

> *Now to a labor, his wages are not counted as a favor or a gift, but as an obligation (something owed him). But to the one who, not working [by the law], trust (believes fully) in Him Who justifies the ungodly, his faith is credited to him as righteousness (the standing acceptable to God."* (Romans 4:4–5 AMP)

Living in Christ is not hard and painful, but letting go and trusting can be. I had placed a huge wedge of law between God and me. I believed that God judged me based upon my obedience, and in order to qualify for his grace, I had to follow the Law perfectly. God wanted me to know that He called me into fellowship with Himself and his Son Jesus. God wanted to show me that I'm no longer under the slavery of law, but I became righteous when I placed my faith in Jesus. I become a daughter:

> *... the Law served [to us Jews] as our trainer, [our guardian, our guide to Christ, to lead us] until Christ [came], that we might be justified (declared righteous, put in right standing with God) by and through faith.* (Galatians 3:24 AMP)

God saved me by grace. He clothed me with the finest robe, the robe of righteousness, and labeled me as his beloved daughter. God wanted me to know He loved me perfectly. I know what it's like to be under the law. I have experience in the impossibility of keeping the law. Mixing law and grace is extremely dangerous. It causes confusion and leaves us feeling unworthy and condemned. When we don't have a clear sense of our complete forgiveness in Christ, we'll constantly be on an emotional seesaw. There will be times we'll feel things between us and God are good because we're not struggling or going through a trial, but, at other times, when we're struggling or in a trial, we'll feel that God is distant, unhappy, and in judgment of us. Our confidence is based in our obedience and not in the perfection and obedience of Christ.

But we are all alike. We are stained with sin and in need of a royal bath. Think about the last New Year's resolution you made. How long did you manage to go before giving in and returning to the old way of life? Trying to come into right standing with God, by our own obedience, is a sure failure. Just like that old resolution, the moment you depend on your own strength, you will fall back in the old way of life. The only way to overcome sin is to come into right standing before God and receive God's righteousness through Christ. Here it is in a nutshell:

Just as one person (Adam) sinned and got us in all this trouble with sin, condemnation and death, another person (Jesus) did it right and got us out of it. But more than just getting us out of trouble, he got us into life! One man (Adam) said no to God and put many people in the wrong; one man (Jesus) said yes to God and gave us right standing with God and life." (Romans 5:18 Paraphrased)

CHAPTER 7

Religious Captivity

I WAS TAUGHT that when I sinned, I lost my salvation. I was taught that my sins separated me from God. Therefore, I saw myself as a powerless sinner, and I couldn't rise above my belief. What we think determines what we do, what we feel, and, ultimately, how we live. The writer of Proverbs wrote, "For as he [a person] thinketh in his heart, so is he" (23:7 KJV). When we think right thoughts, we will live right—as children of the King. But when we think wrong thoughts, we do wrong things and have wrong, unpleasant feelings. The truth is when we are born again, the old sinful nature dies, and our spirit is made alive unto God:

> Therefore if any person is [engrafted] in Christ (the Messiah) he is a new creation (a new creature altogether); the old [previous moral and spiritual condition] has passed away. Behold the fresh and new has come! But all these things are from God, Who through Jesus Christ reconciled us to Himself [received us into favor, brought us into harmony with Himself] and gave to us the ministry of reconciliation [that by word and deed we might aim to bring others into harmony with Him]. (2 Corinthians 5:17–18 AMP)

The Pauline Revelation gives us new insight to the word *redemption*. All of mankind is in need of redemption. Our natural state can be characterized in one word—guilty: "For everyone has sinned; we all fall short of God's glorious standard" (Romans 3:23 NLT). *Redeem* means "to buy back." Christ Jesus bought back, redeemed us, and freed us from guilt. His redemption at the cross included eternal life, forgiveness of sins, and the gift of righteousness. Christ freed us from the law's curse and gave us adoption into God's family. Righteousness is the ability to stand in the Father's presence without a sense of guilt—to have the freedom to stand there without condemnation or sin consciousness. Righteousness comes to the born-again man through faith in Jesus. Acknowledging Christ as Savior and confessing Him as Lord justifies us on the grounds of grace. Our redemption came into effect when God laid upon Jesus our sins and diseases:

Surely He has borne our griefs (sicknesses, weaknesses, and distresses) and carried our sorrows and pains [of punishment], yet we [ignorantly] considered Him stricken, smitten, and afflicted by God [as if with leprosy]. But He was wounded for our transgressions, He was bruised for our guilt and iniquities; the chastisement [needful to obtain] peace and well-being for us was upon Him, and with the stripes [that wounded] Him we are healed and made whole. All we like sheep have gone astray, we have turned everyone to his own way; and the Lord has made to light upon Him the guilt and iniquity of us all. (Isaiah 53: 4–6 AMP)

Jesus was our substitute. God made Christ, who had never sinned, to be the sin offering on our behalf so that we could become righteousness in Him. God accepted His substitutionary sacrifice on our behalf:

He was handed over to die because of our sins, and he was raised to life to make us right with God." (Romans 4:25 NLT)

Our sins were put away once and for all in the body of Christ Jesus. He satisfied the claims of God's Justice. The moment Jesus uttered, "It is finished" (John 19:30 KJV). He went into the belly of the earth (hell) with all authority and power and stripped Satan of his authority. He took back the dominion that was once turned over to him by Adam in the garden. He conquered Satan. He took back the keys to death, hell, and the grave. When Christ rose from the dead, he gave the keys of the kingdom to us. A key represents a badge of authority. Once Satan had the right to bring chaos to Christians' lives; however, he was now rendered powerless. But when Christ rose from the dead, our redemption, dominion and authority became a resolved issue.

Notice, Christ was raised because of our justification. Now, God in His gracious kindness declares us not guilty. We partake of the gift of righteousness when we believe that Jesus shed His blood, sacrificing His life for us. We are found complete in His righteousness:

For God made Christ, who never sinned, to be the offering for our sin, so that we could be made right with God through Christ. (2 Corinthians 5:21 NLT)

What is righteousness? When we received Jesus as our Savior, we received the gift of righteousness, which enables us to reign in life (Romans 5:17 KJV). This righteousness does not come from us (our obedience) but the Lord. When we are established in His righteousness, no weapon formed against us will prosper. But what does being established in righteousness mean? To be established in something is to have that something as your very foundation for security. God wants us to know, be confident, and grow in the revelation that we are righteous by the blood of Jesus—by His perfect sacrifice at the cross (Isaiah 61:10 KJV). We are covered by Jesus' blood. We are cleansed and declared righteous by His obedience. God has clothed us with the robe of righteousness, which was paid for by Jesus' blood. I am not talking about a physical robe made of cloth. I am talking about the robe of righteousness that was on Jesus when He said to the storm, " … 'Peace, be still!' And the wind ceased and there was a perfect calm" (Mark 4:39 NKJV). When we believe that we are righteous because of Jesus' blood, we will experience the benefits of wearing His robe of righteousness:

Bless the Lord, O my soul, and forget not all His benefits; Who forgives all your iniquities, Who heals all your diseases, Who redeems your life from destruction, Who crowns you with lovingkindness and tender mercies, Who satisfies your mouth with good things, So that your youth is renewed like the eagle's. The Lord executes righteousness And justice for all who are oppressed. (Psalm 103:1–6 NKJV)

By the sacrifice of Christ, we are in the family. We no longer have to cower like fearful slaves. Instead, we can approach God with confidence, calling him "Father, dear father." We are God's own children, adopted in his family. Not only are we sons and daughters of God, but, also, we are joint-heirs with Christ. God is actually our Father. The Father has reconciled us to Himself through Christ. The old nature of sinful consciousness (fear) that was ruled by Satan, stopped being. A new nature that is built out of the nature of God (faith) has taken its place. We are now sons and daughters of God. Since we are His children, it's perfectly natural to approach Him with freedom and liberty. The gift of righteousness gives us the privilege to stand in God's presence without sin, guilt, condemnation, or inferiority.

Let me ask you, if I came to you and said I paid off your house mortgage, car note, student loan, or hospital bills, would you still insist on paying those bills? Of course not. Well, then why do we think that we must continue to pay for our sin debt and suffer punishment for sins?

The day Jesus hung on the cross and said, "It is finished," He was announcing our victory. By His blood, He stamped on our debt, "paid in full"; the debt we owed was forever erased from our account. When you look toward the cross, see the cost of your sins and the amazing grace of God, draw near to the throne, and thank him for canceling your debt.

CHAPTER 8

Moving Forward

OUR FAITH GROWS as we act on the Word of God. A great example of this is found in the story about the battle of Jericho, which was won by Joshua and the Israelites. Joshua sent some of his men from Jericho to scout out the city of Ai, east of Bethel, near Beth-aven. The men returned with a report that the town was small, and it wouldn't take more than two or three thousand men to destroy it. When Joshua's men went out, they were soundly defeated. The men of Ai chased them and killed about thirty-six Israelites, who were paralyzed with fear at this turn of events. When Joshua found out what happened, he tore his cloths in dismay, threw dust on his head, and bowed down facing the Ark of The Lord until evening. Then Joshua cried out, "Lord, why did you bring us across the Jordan River if you are going to let the Amorites kill us? What am I to do now that Israel has fled from its enemies? The Lord said, "Get up! Why are you lying on your face like this? Israel sinned and broke my covenant" (Joshua 7:1–11 Paraphrased)!

The Lord told Joshua that when the Israelites conquered Jericho, they were to burn everything in the city that belonged to the people of Jericho, except the silver, gold, brass, and iron. These items were to be brought to the House of the Lord. Joshua had carefully instructed his soldiers and made sure every man knew that these were the orders. Achan was a soldier who disobeyed the orders and hid a beautiful garment and some silver and gold in his tent. Achan felt sure no one else would find out about this. But the Lord knew.

When Joshua went to battle the next time, they were defeated. Joshua fell on his face before the Lord to find out why they were defeated. Defeat was not something that should have happened. Why? The Lord had promised to be with him and defeat his enemy. The Lord told Joshua that Israel had been defeated in battle because someone had disobeyed—they had sinned and had hidden goods in their tent. God also said He would not be with them in battle until the goods were brought forth and the sin dealt with. Joshua lived under the Law of Moses, which taught that God's blessing and presence hinged on man's obedience. When Joshua's men disobeyed, they did not receive mercy; they received judgment. The Law gave strict instructions that the penalty for breaking the law of God was judgment and death.

God knew man's inability to keep the Law. This is why Jesus came! The Law demanded a sacrifice and offering, burnt offerings, and offerings for sin. Jesus said, "I have come down from heaven, not to do My own will, but the will of Him who sent Me" (John 6:38 NLT). The sacrifices under the Law showed that sin tore apart the perfect harmony man once had with God. But Christ's offering for sin would sanctify all mankind through the offering of the body of Jesus Christ once and for all.

Today, we do not live under the rules of the law; we live under the New Covenant of grace. In this New Covenant, we receive blessings, acceptance and the continual presence of God by grace through faith in Christ Jesus. When we sin, God imparts grace, which empowers us to put our past failures behind us and move us forward into victory. Most Christians, today, tend to slip backward into the idea that the acceptance God gives is contingent on our obedience, and if we will do the right things, God will bless us. But we fail to realize that His blessings have been provided as a gift, and gifts aren't given on the basis of merit. God didn't decide to bless us because of how wonderful we are in our performance, but because of how wonderful He is.

Our lives become paralyzed when we approach God in self-righteousness, thinking we must deserve God's acceptance and blessings. Of course, we do not deserve them! But this isn't about us; it's about Christ. We do not earn favor with God; we simply enjoy favor by faith. He's the giver, and we're the receiver. God tells us, "All praise to God, the Father of our Lord Jesus Christ, who has blessed us with every Spiritual blessing in the heavenly realms because we are united with Christ" (Ephesians 1:3 NLT). Fantastic news, right? This means we are forever free from the struggle of trying to stay on God's good side in order for things to go well for us. Our new life is found in Christ alone.

I know it's hard to take in, but it's true. God desires for us to be consumed with the realization that in Jesus Christ, we already have everything we need for time and eternity. The Word of God says, " ... All things whatsoever ye pray and ask for, believe that ye receive them, and ye shall have them" (Mark 11:24 ASV). The statement here is that, if you believe that you already have received your request (that is, of course, in Christ), then "you shall have them."

To believe that you may get something, or that you can get it or even that you will get it, is not faith. Jesus says, "Faith is to believe that you have already got it." Faith says, "God has done it." We did not receive our salvation by trying but by trusting in Jesus. It was by trusting Jesus to forgive our sins and give us His life and making us a brand new creation. The same faith and trust we place in Jesus for our Salvation and forgiveness is the same faith to believe that "All blessings have been given to us freely through Jesus" (Ephesians 1:3 Paraphrased). At the cross Jesus defeated sin and became the curse for us that we would be made rich in Him:

So all who put their faith in Christ share the same blessing Abraham received because of his faith." (Galatians 3:9 NLT)

When we rely on the works of the Law—our obedience—we are under a curse. Clearly, no one who relies on their own righteousness is justified before God because the righteous live by faith. Clearly, rule keeping is not based on faith; on the contrary, it says, "The person who does these things will live by them." Christ redeemed us from the curse of the law by becoming a curse for us. He redeemed us in order that the blessing given to Abraham might come to us when we place our faith Christ Jesus.

CHAPTER 9

A Choice to Make

LET'S LOOK AT the blessing given to Abraham. God told Abram to leave his country, family, and father's home for a land that He would show him. God did not send him off empty-handed; He gave him a promise of an everlasting covenant: The Lord had said to Abram, "Leave your native country, your relatives, and your father's family, and go to the land that I will show you. "I will make you a great nation. I will bless you and make you famous, and you will be a blessing to others. I will bless those who bless you and curse those who treat you with contempt. All the families on earth will be blessed through you" (Genesis 12: 1–3 NLT).

Abraham lived years before the Law was given. He was a sinner, born into sin by the transgression of Adam in the garden, but to enjoy the fruits of God's grace. Abraham was put into right standing with God because he believed in God to make him righteous (Romans 4:9 NLT). When Abraham sinned, he didn't come into judgment like Joshua; he was met with God's overflowing love and grace.

In Genesis, the writer continues with the story of Abraham: Abram left his country and set out for the land of Canaan. A severe famine came to the land, so Abram went down to Egypt. Abram feared for his life because his wife Sarai was so beautiful. He said, "When the Egyptians see you, they will say, 'This is his wife. Let's kill him; then we can have her.' I have a great idea! Let's say you are my sister, then the Egyptians will treat me well because of their interest in you, and my life will be spared" (Genesis 12:10– 13 Paraphrased).

Sure enough, when they arrived in Egypt, everyone spoke of Sarai's beauty. When comforted by the Egyptians, Abram and Sarai followed their plan and lied, saying Sarai was his sister. The King took Sarai into his harem and gave Abram many gifts because of her. But The Lord sent a terrible plague upon Pharaoh's household because of Sarai, Abram's wife. Abram and Sarai both sinned, but God extended grace to them and judgment to Pharaoh. Again, Abraham lied, saying Sarah was his sister. "And Abraham journeyed from there to the South, and dwelt between Kadesh and Shur, and stayed in Gerar. Now Abraham said of Sarah his wife, 'She is my sister.' And Abimelech king of Gerar sent and took Sarah (20:1–3 NLT).

God threatened judgment upon Abimelech for taking Sarah. God came to Abimelech in a dream by night and said to him, "Indeed you are a dead man because of the woman whom you have taken, for she is a man's wife." But Abimelech had not come near her; and he said, "Lord, will You kill an innocent man? Abraham told me, 'She is my sister'? And she, even she herself said, 'He is my brother.' I acted in complete innocence!" And God said to him in a dream, "Yes, I know that you are innocent. For I withheld you from sinning against Me; therefore I did not let you touch her. Now therefore, restore the man's wife; for he is a prophet, and he will pray for you and you shall live. But if you do not restore her, know that you shall surely die you and your entire household" (20:4–8 Paraphrased).

Despite Abraham's failure to trust God in the situation, God was not going to abandon him. He would not let Abimelech touch Sarah. God made a covenant with Abraham promising to curse anyone who came against him. God promises to bless Abraham required nothing of Abraham:

My covenant I will not break, Nor alter the thing that is gone out of my lips. (Psalm 89:34 ASV)

When God promised to give Abraham land, Abraham asked, "… O Sovereign Lord, how can I be sure that I will actually possess it" (Genesis 15:8 NLT)? And as if His word wasn't good enough, God went one step further and made a covenant with Abraham, binding Himself irrevocably to it to reassure His friend that He would do as promised). "And it came to pass, when the sun went down and it was dark, that behold, there appeared a smoking oven and a burning torch that passed between those pieces. On the same day the Lord made a covenant with Abram, saying: 'To your descendants I have given this land, from the river of Egypt to the great river, the River Euphrates; the Kenites, the Kenezzites, the Kadmonites, the Hittites, the Perizzites, the Rephaim, the Amorites, the Canaanites, the Girgashites, and the Jebusites'" (Genesis 15:17–21 Paraphrased). God bound Himself to a covenant with us when He cut it with our substitute and representative, Jesus, at Calvary. "So all who put their faith in Christ share the same blessing that Abraham received because of his faith (Galatians 3:9 NLT).

I lived ten years of my Christian life in a whirlwind of struggle. I struggled in my thought life, which affected my Christian walk. But the moment I called out to God and asked him for understanding of his grace, I began to see the perfection of his love that was demonstrated at the cross. He showed me through his Word how his Son Jesus had borne all my sins, took my punishment for sin, and bore His anger against me. After The Lord showed me the truth, I had a choice to make. I could receive His Word by faith, or I could reject it. I could continue trying to earn His love by my obedience, which is called *self-righteousness,* or I could open my heart to Him and believe the love sacrifice of His Son, Jesus. I could receive his gift of righteousness, or I could reject the gift and continue in a war of struggle.

Are you struggling and feel out of touch with God? When we approach God in our own strength and performance, we quickly become tired of trying to live up to the Christian life. I think it's pretty normal to want to please God with our life, but we understand that God does not demand perfection from us. God is not looking for us to measure up. Look at Abraham; he made many mistakes, but God accepted him. All the Father is asking from us is to believe that the blood of his Son, Jesus, has justified us and has given us peace with God, securing us access into his grace.

CHAPTER 10

Jesus is the Answer

THE TRUTH IS that we are guilty of sin and deserve the penalty of death. Every single day, our flesh is at war with our Spirit. In the Book of Romans, the apostle Paul explained the conflict with our struggles and how to overcome them. He wrote that we died to sin when we died with Christ and we became one with him when God raised him the dead. As a result of our new nature, we can produce a harvest of good deeds for God. Before we came to Christ, we were controlled by our old nature, and sinful desires were at work within us. By Christ's victory, we have been released from the Law and are no longer captive to its power. Now, we can serve God, not in the old way of obeying the letter of the Law, but in the new way of living in the Spirit:

In Christ, the fullness of God lives in a human body, and we are complete through our union with Christ. When we came to Christ, we were circumcised but not of a physical procedure. It was a spiritual procedure—the cutting away of our sinful nature. We were dead to God because of our sins and because our sinful nature was not yet cut away. But God made us alive with Christ! He forgave all our sins. He cancelled the record that contained the charges against us. He took it and destroyed it by nailing it to Christ's cross.

Well then, am I suggesting that the law of God is sinful? Of course not! In fact, it was the law that showed me my sin. I would never have known that coveting is wrong if the law had not said, "You must not covet." But sin used this command to arouse all kinds of covetous desires within me! If there were no law, sin would not have that power. At one time I lived without understanding the law. But when I learned the command not to covet, for instance, the power of sin came to life, and I died. So I discovered that the law's commands, which were supposed to bring life, brought spiritual death instead. Sin took advantage of those commands and deceived me; it used the commands to kill me. (Romans 7:7–11 NLT)

How can we live the new life in Christ? God took an oath that Christ would always be our priest, but he never did this for any other priest. Only to Jesus did he say, "The Lord has taken an oath and will not break his vow. You are a priest forever" (Hebrews 5:6 Paraphrased). Because of God's oath, it is Jesus who guarantees the effectiveness of this better covenant. Jesus remains a priest forever; His priesthood will never end. That is why He is able, once and forever, to save everyone who comes to God through him. He lives forever to plead with God on our behalf.

In the ninth chapter of Hebrews, Paul wrote, "So Christ has now become the High Priest over all the good things that have come. He has entered that greater, more perfect Tabernacle in heaven, which was not made by human hands and is not part of this created world. With his own blood—not the blood of goats and calves—he entered the Most Holy Place once for all time and secured our redemption forever" (11–12 NLT).

That is why he is the one who mediates the new covenant between God and people so that all who are invited can receive the eternal inheritance God had promised them.

What does it mean? Jesus is our high priest and makes intercession for the believer? When we approach God in prayer in Jesus name, Jesus our high Priest adds His perfection to our prayers: " … He lives forever to intercede with God on their behalf" (Hebrews 7:25 NLT). The Word also says,

My little children, these things write I unto you that ye may not sin. And if any man sin, we have an Advocate [intercessor, mediator] with the Father, Jesus Christ the righteous." (1 John 2:1 ASV)

For example, Sue is dating a young man from her work place. Sue likes her boyfriend but feels it's dishonoring to herself and God to give in to her emotions. One evening while attending a party, she compromised her beliefs and gave into her emotions. Later, that evening, she began to feel a heap of condemnation and guilt. She turned to the Lord, received his gift of no condemnation, and embraced his love and forgiveness. The next time Sue was alone with her boyfriend, and the temptation came, she looked to Jesus for strength to abstain from the temptation (feelings, desires); He freely extended grace, which gave her the ability to walk away.

God's grace is the key to overcoming temptation. The next time you find yourself in a compromising situation, look for the supply of God's grace. The moment you call out to God for strength, the Holy Spirit will provide a way out of the bad emotion, and you'll experience the presence of God, which is love, joy, and peace. The only way to exit a temptation is through the door of trust.

CHAPTER 11

Forever a Daughter

I WANTED TO receive my inheritance. I was taught that God would bless me financially if I gave a sacrificial offering. But if I held back my tithes and offerings, I would be robbing God, and I would be cursed:

> *"Bring all the tithes into the storehouse so there will be enough food in my temple. If you do," says the Lord of Heaven's Armies, "I will open the windows of heaven for you. I will pour out a blessing so great you won't have enough room to take it in! Try it! Put me to the test!* (Malachi 3:10 NLT)

I was taught that the responsibility for the blessings of God hung in the balance of my obedience, and I believed it hook, line, and sinker. I was watching television one evening, and the preacher was teaching on the blessings of obedience. At the end of the program, he gave a plea for the viewing audience to partake of the "double blessing." At that time in my life, I believed God for a particular, material item. I wanted God to open the windows of heaven and pour me out a blessing. And I wanted Him to be proud of me. I longed for him to one day look at me and say, "Well done, good, and faithful servant." I had been saving for the item for which I believed. When the preacher shared that God wants us to test him, I decided to give in and send the money I had been saving—one thousand dollars. I immediately went online to make my pledge. After I made my pledge, I felt really happy. I thought, "I sowed my seed, and now I will reap one hundred fold! I bet God is so proud of me—as I patted myself on the back!"

The next day, I checked my online banking and noticed the money had not been withdrawn. I called the ministry I gave to and decided to make my pledge over the phone. I gave the lady my card information, but she returned and said, "I'm sorry your card is declined." How weird, I thought. I had plenty of money in my account. During the evening, the Lord began to share His love. He showed me through his Word that He has accepted and blessed me with every blessing in Christ. He said, "I have not withheld any blessing from you! You do not have to pay for me to take care of your needs and desire. I am your Father. It gives me great joy to give you the kingdom. I know what you need, and I have already provided it to you through my Son" (John 16:24 Paraphrased). I sat in my recliner in total shock!

Then, the Lord shared that He had protected me. He did not allow my pledge to go through because He loved me. He knew my heart's attitude was to honor him; I was just ignorant to the truth of what I had already received in Christ. I will never ever forget that experience. The Lord's grace guarded me from the adversary's attempt to steal from me:

Then Jesus shouted out again, and he released his spirit. At that moment the curtain in the sanctuary of the Temple was torn in two, from top to bottom. The earth shook, rocks split apart." (Matthew 27:50–51 NLT)

Jesus turned to his disciples and said,

"In a little while you won't see me anymore. But a little while after that, you will see me again." Some of the disciples asked each other, "What does he mean when he says, 'In a little while you won't see me, but then you will see me,' and 'I am going to the Father'? And what does he mean by 'a little while'? We don't understand." Jesus realized they wanted to ask him about it, so he said, "Are you asking yourselves what I meant? I said in a little while you won't see me, but a little while after that you will see me again. I tell you the truth, you will weep and mourn over what is going to happen to me, but the world will rejoice. You will grieve, but your grief will suddenly turn to wonderful joy. John 16:16–22 ASV)

Here Jesus reveals to us that by His death and resurrection, we have the privilege to approach God in His name—Jesus—and the Father will give us what we ask.

The Father responds to us because we approach him based on the finished work of His Son. No longer does the Father respond to our works of obedience, but its Christ obedience that gives us all blessings. Jesus said … *I have spoken of these matters in figures of speech, but soon I will stop speaking figuratively and will tell you plainly all about the Father. Then you will ask in my name. I'm not saying I will ask the Father on your behalf, for the Father himself loves you dearly because you love me and believe that I came from God.* (John 16:25–27 ASV)

Even so, Abraham believed God, and it was reckoned to him as righteousness. You can be sure that it is those who are of faith who are sons of Abraham:

And the scripture, foreseeing that God would justify the Gentiles by faith preached the gospel beforehand unto Abraham, saying, In thee shall all the nations be blessed. So then they are of faith are blessed with the faithful Abraham. (Galatians 3:8–9 ASV)

This is powerful truth. Clearly, Jesus is showing us the authority of his name. His name gives us the privilege of throwing off the old garment of self-righteousness and partaking of his divine righteousness:

"Christ redeemed us from the curse of the Law, having become a curse for us; for it is written, "Cursed is every one that hangeth on a tree": that upon the Gentiles might come the blessing of Abraham in Christ Jesus; that we might receive the promise of the Spirit through faith." (Galatians 3:13–14 ASV)

If we receive our inheritance based on our works, it is no longer based on a promise; but God has granted it to Abraham by means of a promise. Abraham is our example. It was by faith that Abraham inherited the promises. Abraham believed that God would keep his promise, and so the whole nation came from one man. Abraham was too old (100-years-old) to have any children, but Abraham never wavered in the promises of God. But he grew in strength in faith, giving glory to God. By faith, men of God overthrew kingdoms, ruled with justice, and received what God had promised them. Their weakness was turned to strength.

Likewise, we who believe enter into God's rest. This Good News has been announced to many, but it did them no good because they didn't believe what God had told them. Only we who believe can enter His place of rest. The place of rest was not in the land of Canaan, where Joshua led the children of Israel. If it had been, God would have not spoken about another day of rest. This new place of rest is awaiting us. All who enter into God's rest will rest from their labor, just as God rested after He created the world.

Through the work of Christ, I have my inheritance. Now that my heart is free from the condemnation, I am free to give to those who are in need. We humans are selfish by nature. Generosity is not something that comes naturally, but is the result of God's grace in our lives. Paul referred to the Corinthian offering as this act of grace. Giving is identified as a gift of the Spirit in Romans 12:8 (NLT). Paul does not command the Roman believers to give. But in their willingness to give, they would reflect the love of Christ to the Christians in Jerusalem. When we see the need of others, we get the opportunity to express the love we have freely received.

Paul explains that giving should come from our free will. We give according to what we have. It isn't important how much we are able to give, God wants us to give what we have, not what we don't have. We should give out of an overflow of love. Our desire should be that others might be relieved. The goal is to have unity! The apostle Paul wrote, "But to have equality [share and share alike], your surplus over necessity at the present time going to meet their want and to equalize the difference created by it, so that [at some other time] their surplus in turn may be given to supply your want. Thus there may be equality, As it is written, He who gathered much had nothing over, and he who gathered little did not lack. (2 Corinthians 8:14-15 AMP). Why did they give? They gave themselves to Christ, which would include a willingness to use all that they had to further His work.

As the Roman believers submitted themselves to Christ, they wanted to participate in this offering. The Book of Acts gives us an example to follow. All the believers were of one heart and mind, and they felt that what they owned was not their own; they shared everything they had. They gave great powerful witness to the resurrection of The Lord Jesus, and God's great grace was upon them all. There was no poverty among them because people who owned land or houses sold them and brought the money to the apostles to give to others in need (Acts 4:32–35). Paul wrote …

Regarding the relief offering for poor Christians that is being collected, you get the same instructions I gave the churches in Galatia. Every Sunday each of you make an offering and put it in safekeeping. Be as generous as you can. When I get there you'll have it ready, and I won't have to make a special appeal. Then after I arrive, I'll write letters authorizing whomever you delegate, and send them off to Jerusalem to deliver your gift. If you think it best that I go along, I'll be glad to travel with them. (1 Corinthians 16:2–4 MSG)

Jesus willingly gave to save us. Jesus became a curse for us so that we would escape the curse and be blessed instead (Galatians 3:12–13).

In the story of the prodigal son, the son states, "I don't deserve to be called your son ever again" He assumed that his relationship to his father was ruined. He thought, "Surely my father is angry with me. I was so demanding and lost my inheritance. I'm such a failure!" Like the Prodigal Son, I approached God as a servant, assuming my failures blocked my way home and, therefore, I remained trapped in a struggle of sin behavior for years. I had been redeemed by the blood of Jesus, but I still saw myself as a servant and not a daughter. A servant isn't a permanent member of the household, but a son remains forever.

My serious lack of understanding concerning God's love caused me to stand outside my Father God's house, knocking, begging, and pleading for forgiveness that I had already been given freely in Christ. Jesus said, "You didn't choose me, remember; I chose you, and put you in the world to bear fruit, fruit that won't spoil. As fruit bearers, whatever you ask the Father in relation to me, he gives you." (John 15:16 MSG).

We were grafted into the vine by faith in Christ's sacrifice. Since we have been grafted into the vine (Christ), we do not have to struggle to receive from our Father God. We are not grafted in to produce our own righteousness, but we are grafted in to partake of Christ's righteousness. His righteousness gives us access to the privileges of being God's children. Christ Jesus, throughout his earthly ministry, showed us the love of the Father. He revealed to us Father God freely meeting needs, healing, giving forgiveness, providing grace and wisdom, overcoming every temptation, and restoring a dead man to life. Jesus told us plainly that He came to reveal the Father and to show us that every gift is from the Father.

After Jesus was raised from the dead, He appeared to the disciples and said, "At that time you won't need to ask me for anything. I tell you the truth, you will ask the Father directly, and he will grant your request because you use my name" (John 16:23 NLT). He continued, "... for the Father himself loves you dearly..." (v. 27 NLT). The more we receive the truth that "in Christ" we have been made righteous and have received all blessing "in Christ," the more we will experience the God-kind of life. In Christ, we have healing, provision, peace, protection, and wisdom, for which has already been paid by his precious blood. We have been forgiven and accepted in the beloved. As I began to see myself through the eyes of the finished work of Christ, I truly saw how beautiful I am. I am the fruit and the glory of His righteousness.

How do you see yourself when you approach the Father? Regardless of what you've done in your past, it is vital that you forgive yourself for everything in your past. God loves you. He is not looking at your past and passing judgment. If God chose to forget your sins and remove them, then I think you ought to do the same.

CHAPTER 12

Quick, Grab the Robe

THE FATHER WASN'T listening to his son's rehearsed speech. He called to the servants, "Quick. Bring the finest robe and dress him. Put the family ring on his finger and sandals on his feet. The father wasn't listening to his son's rehearsed speech of unworthiness. He would have none of it. Instead, he called to his servant to quickly grab his son's cloths of royalty. The father had waited, looking and longingly for his son to come home, and he wasn't going to allow the garment of guilt and condemnation to distort his son's identity any longer. Can you picture it? Likewise, when we come to our senses and turn our hearts home to the Father, he doesn't waste any time. He's not looking for us to wallow in our failure and beg Him for His gift of grace! He isn't waiting for a full and formal apology; He perceives the heart attitude and comes toward us. He runs to us, kisses us, and immediately confirms our right standing as His children (Luke 15).

The robe identifies our right standing with God, the ring signifies our authority, and the sandals distinguish us as a child. Servants did not wear sandals, only family members did. What a beautiful picture of Father God's love for us!

Grace enforces freedom over sin. This wonderful New Covenant through Christ Jesus frees our hearts from guilt, condemnation, and inferiority. No longer do we have to fear God's anger and judgment when we fail. God's Word says, "Let us therefore come boldly to the throne of grace, that we may obtain mercy and find grace to help in time of need" (Hebrews 4:16 NKJV). Mercy means that we do not get the bad things we deserve, such as condemnation, poverty, failure, and even death. But when we come, we'll find grace! Grace means that we get the good things that we do not deserve, such as health, protection, favor, provision, wisdom, peace, and an abundant life. Since we have a High-Priest, Jesus, who is seated at God's right hand interceding for us, let's cling to Him and never stop trusting Him. Today, my life is extremely different. No matter how awful or painful the situation or how chaotic my emotions may be, I choose not to run. I choose not to medicate my pain with the things that gratify my flesh. The old man (woman) no longer exists. I know that repressing pain will not make it go away. Instead, I turn to God with complete honesty, giving Him access into the dark and painful areas of my life. I understand that if I'm going to receive help from God, I have to acknowledge the truth about my condition. I must face up to reality and take off my mask. Trusting God is a process, one that I'm learning daily.

Today, my life is on track. I have peace, love, joy, hope, healing, and a future; I never thought some of these things would be a part of my life. I know I'm God's precious daughter whom He loves. I know I am forgiven. I know my Heavenly Father accepts me. I know I have been made one with Christ Jesus. My willingness to forgive my dad, as well as myself, has freed me, and I'm no longer being held captive to destructive emotions from my past. Sixteen years later, I can openly and honestly express a desire to have a godly husband. But until that day comes, I will keep letting God love me and teach me to give love.

CHAPTER 13

Utter Dependence

LETTING GO AND trusting God is releasing your own understanding and realizing that God has a plan that cannot fail. In other words, it's trusting in the plan that God has made, ultimately, giving up the need to control the situation. This is not an easy thing to do but an imperative step to seeing God for who He is—our loving Father and provider.

It's my heart's desire to help you understand how important it is to trust God and also to offer some advice that may help you on your journey. Trusting God is an essential part of being a Christian; without trust, there cannot be a relationship. How difficult is it to maintain a relationship with another person when you do not trust that person? Well, why would it be any different with God? The answer is, it's difficult to maintain any relationship without trust, and it's the same way with God (Matthew 10:9–10)

Jesus called his twelve disciples and gave them authority to drive out impure spirits and to heal every disease and sickness. Jesus said ...

> *"Don't think you have to put on a fund-raising campaign before you start. You don't need a lot of equipment. You are the equipment...* (MSG). *Don't take any money in your money belts—no gold or silver, or even copper coins. Don't carry a traveler's bag with a change of clothes and sandals or even a walking stick. Don't hesitate to accept hospitality ..."* (NLT).

The heart of Jesus is compelled for His friends, His disciples, to understand that they can trust God to provide all their needs. He knew in order for them to believe, it was necessary for them to step out and experience dependence on the hospitality of others and the Lord for their provision. In another words, they needed to know they could depend on the promises of God. As the disciples followed the words of Jesus, they, indeed, experienced friendly accommodations; they were provided with everything necessary for them. They had both food and raiment and good lodgings in every place; the houses and hearts of men were opened by Christ to receive them.

For example, when I first came to Christ, it was very difficult for me to trust God with my future. I desperately tried to plan out the next five years. But in my attempt, my plans never succeeded. The psalmist wrote, "The steps of a good man are ordered by The Lord" (Psalm 37:23 NKJV). The key was faith in what God had spoken. It's resting in the love of Christ. The Word says, "Jehovah is my shepherd; I shall not want. He maketh me to lie down in green pastures; He leadeth me beside waters of rest" (Psalm 23:1–2 ASV). Just like the sheep do not need to worry about anything because their shepherd takes care of everything, so we also do not need to worry about anything since Christ Jesus is our shepherd.

Fear of the unknown held me captive for many years, but I was determined in my heart to trust God and break the stronghold. I wish I could tell you that it was easy, that I had an encounter with God and boom! I wish I could say, "I was free from fear," but, that wouldn't be true. The truth is that it was extremely painful. I thought the problem was fear of the unknown, but the Lord revealed to me that it was much deeper. I was broken inside because I didn't believe He loved me. I knew He was my God, but like we say in Texas, "When the dirt hit the road," I feared He wouldn't come through for me. The change took place inside my heart when the Lord revealed to me that He loves me as much as He loves Jesus. He showed me that through His Word, I've been made one with Jesus.

Through the work of Christ, all requirements of the Law have been fulfilled, and, therefore, I've been made the righteousness of God in Christ. My heart was flooded with love, but it was my experiences that brought about trust. I've experienced God, instantly, providing. Also, I've waited for days and sometimes weeks and there still are some prayer requests for which I continue to trust God. In some ways, "waiting upon the Lord" is the hardest part of trusting. It's not the same as "waiting around." It's putting yourself, with utter vulnerability, in the hands of God. When I'm tempted to give up, I'm drawn to the words of Jesus:

> *So don't worry about these things, saying, "What will we eat? What will we drink? What will we wear?" These things dominate the thoughts of unbelievers, but your heavenly Father already knows all your needs. Seek the Kingdom of God above all else, and live righteously, and he will give you everything you need. So don't worry about tomorrow, for tomorrow will bring its own worries. Today's trouble is enough for today."* (Matthew 6: 31–34 NLT)

It's made a big difference in my heart to know I can lean upon Jesus; it gives me peace and hope.

However, I still have days when I struggle because I can't see the provision. And Satan would love for me to doubt God's Love, but greater is He who lives in me than he that's in the world because God loves me. Even when my heart goes into panic-planning mode, the Holy Spirit gently nudges me to return to the place of rest. I believe I will always be in school, learning the lesson of trust, and I'm okay with that. It's great to experience a miracle, but for me, the greatest miracle is learning to live a lifestyle of trust.

I want to know I can trust God to fight my battles, provide, heal my body, bring restoration in my relationships, and fulfill His purpose and calling in my life. I've lived many years depending on myself and other people, and it has left me disappointed. God has made a promise to me in Romans: " … Whoever believes on him will not be put to shame" (10:11 NKJV). The journey isn't always easy, but I can honestly express the faithfulness of God. I'm learning that every painful experience has purpose. And when I allow God to reveal his love in the midst of heartache and difficulty, I'm never disappointed. For those who turn to Him will never be disappointed.

Being a needy person can often be viewed as having a very unhealthy behavior; otherwise known as clingy. Depending on others too much is not attractive or pleasant to be around. When we're constantly asking someone else's opinion on the most basic parts of life, this habit can indicate a lack of self-confidence and relying too much on others. The Word declares . . .

Like newborn babies, you must crave pure spiritual milk so that you will grow into the full experience of salvation. Cry out for this nourishment, now that you have had a taste of the Lord's kindness. You are coming to Christ, who is the living cornerstone of God's temple. He was rejected by people, but he was chosen by God for great honor. And you are living stones that God is building into his spiritual temple. What's more, you are his holy priest. Through the mediation of Jesus Christ, you offer spiritual sacrifices that please God. (1Peter 2:2–5 NLT)

The Lord showed me a picture of a baby bird sitting in a nest, crying out for food. The bird was completely helpless and waiting on its parent to bring its supply. The Lord began to share with me that this picture was indeed how he desired his children to look toward him in utter dependence. There's a saying that the squeaky wheel gets the grease, and in a sense, it's true for us as well. Within a nest of baby birds, parent birds tend to offer more food to those chicks that are calling out the loudest and most insistently. For baby birds, if you want more attention at feeding time, raise a bigger ruckus than your siblings. The extra food means that those baby birds that call out the loudest have more nutrition and grow fastest. These birds will likely be better able to compete for food and mates when they are on their own:

And now, just as you accepted Christ Jesus as your Lord, you must continue to follow him. Let your roots grow down into him, and let your lives be built on him. Then your faith will grow strong in the truth you were taught, and you will overflow with thankfulness. (Colossians 2:6–7 NLT)

The other key benefit of baby birds calling out for food is that they are exercising and developing the muscles and other apparatus required to sing. Why do birds sing? Birds' songs are important for claiming and defending territory and attracting a mate. Like many of the instinctive behaviors exhibited by babies of all sorts, the crying of baby birds is an important part of their early development in many respects.

The world in which we live says this behavior of being needy comes off as toxic, and others tend to run the other direction from co-dependence, but the

Lord would like us to know that He welcomes our needy behavior. God desires us to cry out daily for growth, strength, wisdom, supply, and direction. When we rest knowing God welcomes our neediness, we relax and see Him as our Father. Many people feel they should not ask God, continually, for the things they need, want, or desire. But God told us in His Word that we should not get tired of asking Him for the things we want from Him: "For everyone who asks, receives. Everyone who seeks, finds. And everyone who knocks, the door will be opened" (Matthew 7:8 NLT).

The prodigal son returned home, trusting that his father would at least treat him as a servant. When he opened himself up and trusted his father, he was met with affirmation of his father's love, forgiveness, and acceptance. We must do the same. We may feel completely helpless, but it's in this moment of trust that God's presence holds us up and gives us strength. I never thought it could be safe to be in a co-dependent relationship with someone. I never thought I could be completely honest and love someone so much until I met Jesus. And I never knew someone would love me, unconditionally. The invitation to need Him allows me to open up even more to share my feelings and desires. My need for God allows me to raise a big ruckus and say loudly, "I need you, God. I need your grace. I need my best friend." The most amazing symbolism aspect of the picture the Lord showed me is that when the bird cries out, it's actually developing its muscles for singing. I love that He wants me to need Him.

CHAPTER 14

It's Safe to Let Go

A FRIEND OF mine recently asked me, "How are you able to remain so confident in the Lord? These kinds of hard situations you've faced would normally wipe out another's faith in God." The strength of my confidence is my understanding that it's safe to be weak. I believe God wants to bring each of His children to a place of dependence. Before I could cross over and rest in God's love, I had to come to the end of myself and recognize that I will never accomplish anything in my own strength. **And to "try" is nothing more than a religious performance.** For example, when I had been crushed under the weight of need, I had to reach the point to express fully, "I cannot do it because it's impossible. God only You can." Before we can enter the land of grace, which flows with milk and honey, it's necessary for us to come to the point where we realize that it isn't just hard to live the abundant life Jesus promised us, it is impossible to do it in our own strength. Only when we give up our own efforts, and allow the life of Christ Himself to live His life through us, will we experience his grace to get the job done.

A question many people often ask themselves when facing tough circumstances is, "WHY did God forsake me?" Why would He allow a zealous missionary, pastor, mom, or student to be overwhelmed by adversity? Why would God allow the apostle Paul to face such extreme burdens that he despaired of life? The Bible gives us a clear answer to the question. Second Corinthians 1:9 (NLT) says, " … as a result, we stopped relying on ourselves and learned to rely only on God, who raises the dead." Having trust in ourselves is the default settings of this world, but it's not the setting of the Kingdom. It's thinking that the "old man" had before he was born again. God's perspective stands in great contrasts to the opinions of man. We can see throughout the entire Bible that God's design for man is to be completely dependent upon God's love to oversee his life. He loathes our independence; instead, He desires that we become like little children who recognize our need to totally depend upon Him.

Relinquishing control of my life hasn't been easy. But I've experienced that it's the only way to enjoy God's amazing grace. For me, total abandonment to self-sufficiency is a process. In Luke 9:23, Jesus said, "Whoever wants to be my disciple must deny themselves and take up their cross daily and follow me (Paraphrased)." I'll be honest; it was absolutely scary to surrender the control of my life. But as one who is learning daily to let go, I can say it's such a joy and great rest to not be under any weight and to know deep within my heart that I have a Heavenly Father who wants to care for my every need. In Isaiah 30:18, the writer stated, "Therefore the Lord will wait, that He may be gracious to you; And therefore he will be exalted, that He may have mercy on you. For the Lord is a God of Justice; Blessed are all those who wait for Him. (NKJV)." And, then, Luke declared, "So don't be afraid, little flock. For it gives your Father great happiness to give you the kingdom" (12:32 NLT).

If you are gripping tightly to the ropes of control, I want to tell you it's safe to let go. If you are willing to cross over, then step into the water by abandoning yourself and everything you think to accomplish into the loving arms of God. Step forward in God's rest and allow Him to reveal to your heart His love, which can never fail:

Therefore, since we are surrounded by such a huge cloud of witnesses to the life of faith, let us strip off every weight that slows us down, especially the sin that so easily trips us up. And let us run with endurance the race God has set before us. We do this by keeping our eyes on Jesus, the champion who initiates and perfects our faith. Because of the joy awaiting him, he endured the cross, disregarding its shame. Now he is seated in the place of honor beside God's throne. Think of all the hostility he endured from sinful people; then you won't become weary and give up.
(Hebrews 12:1–3 NLT)

We're safe in his love. The prophet wrote, "I am holding you by your right hand—I, the LORD your God" (Isaiah 41:13 Paraphrased).

When my heart becomes restless wondering and worrying, I'm reminded to stay seated and rest in the Lord. When we make a decision to trust God, fear will always come. Fear reminds me of the game, chicken. Fear's goal is to drive us to swerve off course. Fear wants us to panic? Fearful thoughts are sent for one purpose to distract us from seeing our Heavenly Father's love. Thoughts of yesterday or tomorrow come to condemn our heart. I think the voice of condemnation can be summed up into these words, "What are you going to do!" Notice that the lie places YOU in the hot seat, carrying all the responsibility. We must reject this lie! Our Father God has conquered all the problems we'll face. He said …

"Are you tired? Worn out? Burned out on religion? Come to me. Get away with me and you'll recover your life. I'll show you how to take a real rest. Walk with me and work with me- watch how I do it. Learn the unforced rhythms of grace. I won't lay anything heavy or ill- fitting on you. Keep company with me and you'll learn to live freely and lightly." (Matthew 11:28–30 MSG)

As long as we take the liar's bait and carry the responsibility, we'll feel abandoned by God. But this is so far from truth.

God loves us so much! The apostle Paul wrote these words: "We have righteousness as our weapon, both to attack and to defend ourselves" (2 Corinthians 6:7 Paraphrased). Change the lie around by casting your cares onto The Lord, and boldly declaring, "I am not doing to a darn thing, Satan! And I do not have to because Jesus loves me and has already defeated this situation, giving me victory. Thank you for reminding me the battle has been won."

We are not chickens. We are eagles. Eagles rise higher than the circumstances. Eagles know that, above the clouds, the sun is always shining! In order to see the sun shining, we must get a higher perspective. We are made to soar. We must stretch our wings of faith and rise higher to the position of rest. God can be trusted to keep His promises! Choose to wait upon The Lord. Choose to ask for His help in every situation. And choose to believe He loves you and will work out His prefect plan of good in your life.

There's no specific level that our faith has to reach before God gives us what we're asking for. God has already given to us all things that pertain to life and godliness. Yes, the Father of our Lord Jesus Christ has blessed us with every spiritual blessing in the heavenly realms because we are united with Christ (Ephesians 1:3). We must NOT fix our eyes on the amount of faith we think we have. But we must fix our eyes on the One who loves us, who's already given us what we need. It's not our ability to have faith in our faith, but it's faith in the person of Jesus. Jesus is the author and finisher of our faith. The cross has secured our help. When we come to God, we must come to Him, believing that He wants to meet our expectation.

One more essential truth that we must believe is that God's ability equals His willingness. If we recognize that God has the ability (after all, he created the heavens and earth) but do not believe that He is willing, our unbelief will defeat the promises of God in our lives. We must believe that what God says, He is willing to do; He is able to do. The converse is also true; we must believe that what God says He is able to do, He is willing to do. Any time anyone tells us that God can or cannot do something, we must look to His Word to know the truth.

Men will exhibit unwillingness but not God. Men may see a need but be unwilling to help. Men may also be willing to help but lack the resources to help. If I needed to paint my house and you had a spray gun, you could come to me and say, "I can help you with your house, but I don't want to." You have the ability but not the willingness. If you don't have a spray gun or paint brush and come to me willing to help but do not have the resources, you cannot help. God is not this way. What God says is available from His Word, He is able to do, and He is also willing to do. We are His masterpiece, created in Christ Jesus (Ephesians 2:10). We are His children, called before the foundations of the World (Psalm 139).

Many Christians are under the impression that God gives according to our actions. If we are *good enough*, He gives us our health or meets our needs; and if we are not, He punishes us. Or if we work so much for the Lord, He'll give us a reward. But what does God say? We always need to get back to His Word; it is the only way we will truly know:

For as many as are the promises of God, they all find their Yes [answer] in Him [Christ]. For this reason we also utter the Amen (so be it) to God through Him [in His Person and by His agency] to the glory of God. (2 Corinthians 1:20 AMP)

While Jesus was in one of the towns, a man came along who was covered with leprosy. When the man saw Jesus, he fell with his face to the ground and begged him, "'Lord, if you are willing, you can heal me and make me clean.' Jesus reached out and touched him. 'I am willing,' he said. 'Be healed!' And instantly the leprosy disappeared" (Luke 5:12–13 NLT).

What is God's willingness and ability here? God is willing to give grace and glory, no good will He withhold. We must immerse ourselves in His truths to the extent that we know and believe Him so that we may trust in Him and walk in the blessing He purchased:

God is not a man, that he should lie; Neither the son of man, that he should repent: Hath he said, and will he not do it? Or hath he spoken, and will he not make it good?" (Numbers 23:19 ASV)

What God says in His Word He means; when He says He gives freely, He will not withhold any good; bless those that trust in Him. We can take Him at His Word. God never lies; if we doubt anything from the Word of God, we are insinuating that He is a liar. We can rely on His truths completely. No matter the circumstances, no matter the conditions, no matter the facts, nothing is too hard for God.

All of us desire to walk by faith, yet we know so little about the subject. Faith is not something we can work up or have in hand that we take out and use whenever we like. No, faith is a gift of God or fruit of the spirit. The source or origin of faith remains the same—it's a gift of God. If we are in a situation and we find ourselves crying over and trying to have faith, we must stop it. I have found myself, over the years, trying to work to earn faith. But I can honestly say each time I found myself at the end of myself, crying out to God for mercy to intervene, He did. Through the years, I have learned that anytime I focus on my ability to have faith in my faith, I'm preoccupied with myself and have failed to see Jesus in his finished work.

Years ago, I was asked by a good friend how to have faith. I told her, "For me, faith means trusting God. If we want to operate in faith, then, we trust God." In Romans 10:17, we find that "faith comes by hearing, and hearing by the Word of God" (NKJV). We have the capability to believe, but faith is a gift given by God so we can receive all the benefits Jesus paid for on the cross. Belief is in the realm of what is seen (the five senses), but faith is in the "unseen." Faith calls for those things in which we believe to come into the "seen."

God has given to every man the measure of faith (Romans 4:17 NLT). This faith was imparted to us to believe on The Lord Jesus and accept him as Lord. And this same measure is within us all to receive the grace and blessed favor of God. As we hear about the finished works of Jesus, we begin to exchange *our* thoughts, ideas, and beliefs, and opinions for *God's* thoughts, God's beliefs, and God's opinions. By lining up our thinking to the Word our thoughts will come into agreement with what grace has already provided, and we'll experience the abundant life Jesus died and paid for on the cross:

> *By the communication (release or transfer) of thy faith may become effectual (to work or produce) "by the acknowledging" of every good thing which is in you in Christ Jesus."* (Philemon 1:6 Paraphrased)

By acknowledging the good, which is in you in Christ, your faith will respond to what grace has already provided and made available.

CHAPTER 15

Accepted in the Beloved

UNDERSTANDING OUR POSITION in Christ does not mean we will no longer face temptations. But now, when the adversary comes, we have a firm footing to stand against his attacks.

Paul reveals in the Book of Galatians that our salvation comes by faith alone, not by rule keeping. The Father sent his Son to redeem us out of the mentality of slavery by becoming our sin substitute. In Galatians 3, the apostle Paul shows the relationship between the promise of God and the Law of God. Paul highlights the fact that the promise was given to Abraham 430 years before the Law was given through Moses. Paul makes it clear that although he was against rule keeping, he was not against the Law itself. God's intention in giving the Law was good. In fact, God intended for all of us to have a spiritual journey by first passing through the Law in order to enter into the land of promise. Paul said ...

But when the fullness of the time came, God sent forth his Son, born of a woman, born under the law, that he might redeem them that were under the law, that we might receive adoption of sons. And because ye are sons, God sent forth the Spirit of his Son into our hearts, crying, "Abba! Father! So that thou art no longer a bondservant [slave], but a son; and if a son, then an heir through God. (Galatians 4:4–7 ASV)

As I responded to the Father Grace, the struggle to give into temptation lost its power. I had spent years convincing myself that I was a lesbian. I looked to God and blamed Him for my choices. I blamed Him for my shame. I blamed

Him for my pain. When I looked into his Word, I didn't see the supply, but the demand. The more I read, the more I realized how sinful I was:

> ... *I would never have known that coveting is wrong if the law had not said,* *"You must not covet." But sin used this command to arouse all kinds of covet-* *ous desires within me! If there were no law, sin would not have that power.* (Romans 7:7–8 NLT)

Sinful thoughts were dominating me, and I didn't know how to get free. I tried really hard not to think sinful thoughts. The harder I tried, the stronger it got. Would freedom be a reality for me? The Gospel of John says, "If you continue in God's Word, you will know the truth, and the truth will set you free (John 8:32 NLT). I continued in God's word, but I remained wrapped in a cycle of struggle. I rebuked every sinful thought, but the thoughts just bounced right back and condemned me. For example, when a lustful thought ran through my mind, Satan would instantly charge me, "guilty." He'd say, "I thought you were saved. Why, a child of God doesn't think impure thoughts. See, you are a lesbian. God doesn't love you."

For what the Law could not do, in that it was weak through the flesh, God sending his own Son in the likeness of sinful flesh, and for sin, "condemned sin in the flesh" (Romans 8:3 ASV). The likeness of sinful flesh simply means that Jesus suffered as though He was a bondservant under condemnation of sin for mankind. When sinful thoughts rise up, it cannot condemn us before God; it has no more power to separate us from God. Sin was condemned at the cross. Jesus Christ came "in the likeness of sinful flesh." He was tempted in all the same points—desires, feelings, and temptations—without sin. He was perfectly man, like us. God sent his Son Jesus to the cross to destroy sin's control over us by giving Him as a sacrifice for our sins.

Therefore, we who receive the nature of God are now controlled by the Spirit. Since Christ now lives within us, even though our sinful nature is hostile to God, our spirit is alive because we have been made right with God. The Spirit of God's grace empowers us to embrace righteous living. There is freedom from the old man. It becomes a reality in our lives only as we understand the sacrifice of Christ and God's love. As we understand this truth—that our sin was condemned in the body of Christ—all sinful thoughts that rise up will be brought under foot. For it was upon the cross that God judged, condemned, punished, and passed sentence upon it by the suffering and death of his Son Jesus. Because our sins have been condemned, judged in the body of Christ, our sins cannot be visited and punished.

For God to condemn us when we sin would be to punish sin twice—to punish it first in our Representative (Jesus), and then in the represented (us). When we believe God judges our sins, we're actually stating that the sacrifice of Jesus was not good enough to cleanse us. But God, having once condemned sin in the person of Jesus Christ, having accepted the sacrifice, and forever viewing Him as the perfect Representative for his people, cannot condemn sin again in our persons. Through the sacrifice of Christ Jesus, God has declared us not guilty, thus freeing us to embrace our everlasting salvation:

For Christ also suffered once for sins, the just for the unjust, that He might bring us to God, being been put to death in the flesh but made alive in the spirit." (1 Peter 3:19 ASV)

Satan loves it when we loath in our flesh. He comes with accusations in attempt for us to yield our heart to his lies. When we yield to thoughts that contradict the Kingdom of God, we give Satan the materials to build a stronghold in our minds. If we do not know the truth—that our new nature in Christ is free from responding to Satan's impulses in the flesh—we'll feel condemned in our heart and begin to take on the old man's behavior.

For example, a lustful thought runs through your mind; immediately Satan comes to accuse you. Maybe you entertained the thought; maybe you didn't. His next attempt is to attack your thoughts with guilt and judgment. If he can get you to yield to his lies and receive condemnation, your actions will begin to rebel in an attempt to cover the shame you feel. Perhaps, you didn't yield to Satan's lie, but you felt trapped in the lie that your sinful thoughts define your desires and identity.

The truth is, God does not shame or identify us with sinful thoughts. Sinful thoughts are either sent from Satan or it is sin in our flesh, which stirs up evil desires. Sin in the flesh was condemned in the body of Christ. To lay claim, accepting the attraction in the flesh as one's desire or identity, is to honor the kingdom of darkness above the blood of Christ. God does not identify us with the old man any longer; we are identified in Christ Jesus alone. No longer are we sinners, but we are now righteous children of God. Our weapon against "sin conscious" is our new standing with God—being more aware of sin, guilt, imperfections, and condemnation than our right standing with God through the blood of Christ. The Father sees in Christ. We stand before Him without fault in His eyes. Paul wrote, "Even before he made the world, God loved us and chose us in Christ to be holy and without fault in his eyes (Ephesians 1:4 NLT). Sin no longer has the power to accuse, condemn, or separate us from God's love, which is revealed in Christ. We have been made the righteousness of God in Christ. Therefore, there is no condemnation to those in Christ. Why? It is because the law of the Spirit of Christ Jesus has set us free from the law of sin and of death.

Today, God does not condemn us for our sins if we are in Christ Jesus. Jesus is our safe place—our place of rest. In Christ, there is freedom from the entanglement of sin. The dominion of sin has been broken, and its defeat is sure when we rely on the blood of Christ for our wholeness.

Because I didn't fully understand my position in Christ, I bought into Satan's lies, accepting lustful thoughts as my identity and, therefore, condemned myself. I thought, "It's true!" The Word says, "Everyone who sins is a slave. And a slave is not a permanent member of God's family" (John 8:34 Paraphrased).

When I failed, I didn't need any outside help to condemn me because I used God's Word against myself. Satan knows the Word of God, and he will twist it to condemn us.

Jesus went from Galilee to the Jordan River to be baptized by John…. As Jesus came up out of the water, the heavens opened, and He saw the Spirit of God descending like a dove and settling on Him. And a voice from heaven said, "This is my beloved Son, and I am fully pleased with Him" (Matthew 3:13, 16 Paraphrased).

Then Jesus was led into the wilderness by the Holy Spirit to be tempted by the devil. The devil came and said to him, "If you are the Son of God, change these stones in loaves of bread." But Jesus told him, "No! The scripture says. "People need more than bread for their life; they must feed on every word of God." Notice, the devil's temptation; the devil's temptation was an attempt for Jesus to question his position as a child. He just heard His father say, "This is my 'beloved' Son in whom I am well pleased." (4:1–6 Paraphrased)

The devil said, "If you are a Son of God." The devil purposefully left out 'beloved. If the devil can convince us that sinful behavior puts us outside the Father's house and that God is angry with us when we sin, then his temptation will succeed. But the moment we understand that we are the beloved sons and daughters of God through the blood of Jesus, temptations will fail. Now, when a sinful thought runs through my mind, and Satan comes to charge me, "guilty," I reject the thought and his accusations with confirming my righteousness in Christ. In myself, I'm not perfect, but God has made me perfectly righteous in His sight by placing me in Christ. God got rid of all I used to be; He ended my old life by giving me a new life in Christ.

When we walk away from reading or hearing God's Word and feel the load of responsibility to carry out the Word, we have failed to understand the Father's love letter. God doesn't give us a set of rules to follow in order for our day to be a success. His purpose is to remind us that He loves us, He's with us, and His grace is present to straighten any rough spots in our day.

For me, the Word helps me see there isn't a problem that's big enough to outsmart or overpower God's love for me. I'm going to personalize a passage. I hope the eyes of your heart will see Father God's care and love for you!

I, your Heavenly Father send you Grace and peace! I have blessed you with every blessing in heaven because you belong to My beloved Son, Jesus. Before I created the world, I loved you. I chose you in Christ to be holy, and I see you without fault in My eyes. My unchanging plan has always been to adopt you into My family by bringing you to Myself through My Son, Jesus. And this gave Me great pleasure. I purchased your freedom through the blood of My Son, and your sins I have forgiven. I shower you with My kindness. I have poured My wisdom and understanding on you. My purpose is that you will trust in Christ and believe I have identified you as My own child. I have given the Holy Spirit as My guarantee to you that I gave you a glorious inheritance in Christ. (Ephesians 1:3–14 paraphrased)

We are empowered to overcome every temptation when our hearts are at rest in the Father's love. We have victory in this life because God loves us. We overcome all struggles in the flesh by leaning upon the indwelling power of the Holy Spirit. We must bring every thought captive into the obedience of Christ. This means the cross of Christ is now the mirror that reflects our identity:

But we all, with unveiled face, beholding as in a mirror the glory of the Lord, are transformed into the same image from glory to glory, even as from the Lord, the Spirit. (2 Corinthians 3:18 AMP)

I stayed defeated because I was beholding a set of rules. As I looked into the fullness of the law, I felt shame and ran away from God. A friend shared with me a story of a young woman who came to Christ for forgiveness of sins but could not give up her eating disorder. She felt it was wrong and sinful. She tried and tried to stop, but the more she tried, the more she failed. She suffered great shame and condemnation because of her eating disorder. She attended classes on how to stop. My friend tried to tell her that she was too hard on herself, but she felt like a total failure as a Christian. The young woman felt the only way she would be worthy for God's forgiveness is to be perfect. She beat herself up when she made a mistake; the pressure became so unbearable that she wished she could die. The struggle to overcome was nowhere in sight. One day, right in the middle of her struggle, she cried out to God for help. Jesus spoke words of grace into her life. When she received the gift of no condemnation, she was freed from the addiction. At the throne of grace, Jesus defends us and guarantees that all the benefits of the cross are ours. Jesus assures our salvation, healing, and deliverance.

We are transformed into the same image as we behold the glory of the Lord: "For God, who said, 'Let there be light in the darkness,' has made this light shine in our hearts so we could know the glory of God that is seen in the face of Jesus Christ" (2 Corinthians 4:6 NLT). The glory of God is seen in the face of Jesus.

The only way I was going to experience the new life in Christ was by looking away from me and beholding my new image. Jesus is the reflection of the new me. As Jesus is, so am I in this world (1 John 4:17 Paraphrased). I am a new creation, old things have passed away and behold all things have become new. I am the glory of Jesus. Jesus is a child of God, and so am I. Jesus is the righteousness of God, so I am the righteousness of God. God is fully pleased with Jesus, so God is fully pleased with me.

Now, when the adversary comes, I have legal grounds as a child of God to put him in his place. When he comes with accusations of condemnation, I can point to Jesus, and say, "Devil, stop it! Go check Jesus out because as He is, so am I." God does not condemn us today because more than 2,000 years ago, He judged our sins at the cross. God wants us to see ourselves the way He sees us—righteous in Christ. When we sin, He wants us to look away from ourselves and remember that Jesus' blood was shed to continually cleanse us from all unrighteousness (1 John 1:7).

The Lord said to Moses and Aaron: take a lamb and slaughter it at midnight. Then take some of the blood and put it on the sides and tops of the doorframes of the house where the lamb is eaten. When I see the blood, I will pass over you. No destructive plague will touch you (Exodus 12:1–13). The blood on the doorframe was foreshadowing of what Christ would do for us when he shed his blood for our sins. The death sentence, wrath and judgment for our sins, passed over us onto Christ. When the Lord sees the blood of Christ, judgment and condemnation are prevented from coming in. Our right standing with God is permanent. God can justify those in Christ who are still in a sinning state because our justification is "a gift" by His grace through the redemption of Christ Jesus. Our sins were imputed to Christ's account, and his righteousness standing with the Father has been imputed to our account.

God took an oath that Christ would always be a priest, but he never did this for any other priest. Only to Jesus did he say, " ... The Lord has taken an oath and will not break his vow. You are a priest forever'" (Hebrews 7:21 Paraphrased). Because of God's oath, it is Jesus who guarantees the effectiveness of this better covenant. Jesus remains a priest forever; his priesthood will never end. Therefore, he is able, once and forever, to save everyone who comes to God through him. He lives forever to plead with God on your behalf. The writer of the Book of Hebrews says that Jesus has now become the high priest over all the good things that have come. He entered that great, perfect sanctuary in heaven, not made by human hands and not part of this created world. Once and for all time He took blood into the most holy place, but not the blood of animals. He took his own blood, and with it, He secured our salvation forever. By the power of the eternal Spirit, Christ offered himself to God as a perfect sacrifice for our sins (9:11–27).

Has the voice of condemnation come to try to separate you from the Father's embrace? God's grace is not weakened by our sin. In fact, He said, "… for when I am weak, then am I strong" (2 Corinthians 12:10 ASV). It's in the midst of our struggles that His grace will display how powerful the Father's love is for us. The next time you find yourself feeling guilty because you sinned, look up and grab hold of the Lord's outstretched hand. He will take the struggle from you and, in exchange, fill your heart and mind with his perfect peace, reminding you that you're His child. No matter how many times we fail, God will always be there to pick us up.

CHAPTER 16

I Remember their Sins
No More

THE PERFECTION OF Christ gives us continual acceptance, blessings, and love. We are perfected forever in Christ. Our assurance must be based solely on Christ's work, not anything we do. The blessings of the New Covenant are ours, apart from works or penance; it comes solely by faith and by grace. Since Christ Jesus has perfected us forever through his death and resurrection, we can approach the throne of grace with confidence to receive mercy and find grace in the time of need. All praises to him who loves us, and has freed us from our sins by shedding His blood for us. He has made us His Kingdom and his Priests who serve before God His Father (Revelation. 1:5–6). Let's come and drink the water of life without charge, for Jesus is coming back soon:

Blessed are those who wash their robes so they can enter through the gates of the city and eat the fruit from the tree of life!" (Revelation 22:14 ASV)

We must remember that we are God's children only because of God's mercy and His faithful love for us. Our good behavior or religious achievements will not add anything to our salvation. In Christ, we are no longer slaves, but children of God. God loves us as much as He loves His own Son. He accepts us as He accepts Jesus. I am who I am only by the grace of God. And the blessings (favor, love, acceptance, and forgiveness) we receive as God's children are what make us live day-to-day in spite of the many challenges we face. The Father has sent the indwelling person—the Holy Spirit—to help us to have intimate fellowship with God our Father. By Him, we can call God, "Abba, Father!" The Holy Spirit is the power of God that works within us, conforming us into the image of Christ. The Holy Spirit is the deposit guaranteeing us an eternal inheritance. I once thought the Holy Spirit was the bell that went off pointing out my failures and passing judgment upon my heart. But Jesus says that the role of the Holy Spirit is to reveal to us that we have been made complete in Christ. He convicts us of our righteousness. When we fail, He points us back to the cross where are sins were forgiven and put away.

John stated, "Dear friends, we are already God's children, but he has not yet shown us what we will be like when Christ appears. But we do know that we will be like him, for we will see him as he really is" (1 John 3:2 NLT). In this way, love is made complete among us so that we will have confidence in the Day of Judgment because in this world, we are like him. The offering for our sins was purchased by Christ. We cannot add to that satisfaction. Justification is offered freely to all who embrace Christ by faith. No other sacrifices are needed.

God said, "I will be merciful and gracious toward their sins, and I will remember their deeds of unrighteousness no more" (Hebrews 8:12 Paraphrased). Does God forget? Does the Almighty God suddenly have a lapse in His memory? NO! God is very much aware of every sin we commit. The forgetting of God is a relational forgetting. That is, He remembers it no more against us. God forgave our sins at the cross; He no longer holds them against us. He bears no grudges. He harbors no lingering hostility because on the cross, Jesus took all our sins. He took all God's anger against us and the punishment, which our sins deserve. Therefore, we can never be separated from receiving God's love and continual forgiveness. Forgiveness has been paid for; it just needs to be accepted.

We should not go back to any form of legalism. We should remain in Christ by remembering God's grace and enjoying the full privileges we have as God's children—peace, freedom, joy, love, kindness, faithfulness, goodness, and self-control—which cannot be taken away from us. We are no longer slaves but children. My hope is that you will receive your gift of righteousness and realize the Father has rolled out the red carpet for us through Christ. We are children of God. We have a relationship with God through faith in Christ. We are completely forgiven and deeply loved in the beloved!

God made four stunning promises to us after He prophesied the atoning sacrifice Jesus would make for our sins: 1) I will never abandon you; 2) I will never be angry with you again; 3) I will remain loyal to you; and 4) My covenant of blessing will never be broken. Our sin debt has been paid in full. Those feelings of unworthiness, guilty, and condemnation, which have held us back from partaking of God's love and acceptance, have been put away in Christ.

The love and blessings of the Father are not based on our efforts; it's not about us anymore. All requirements have been met in Christ. It would be kind of me to share my view, but these promises are not from me. They come straight from God's Word. When we are born again, we qualify for all these blessings. The only thing that can keep us from experiencing them is our refusal to believe what God has spoken. I would like to encourage you, take the Father's words of promise into your heart and allow your heart to experience the rest that's been available since God created the world.

CHAPTER 17

A Song in Heaven

Kill the calf we have been fattening. My beloved son is home; it's time to rejoice.
Prepare for a celebration tonight in my son's honor. My son is back home
(my interpretation of scripture) (Luke 15:24–25).

THERE IS A great celebration and rejoicing in heaven over one sinner who repents than over ninety-nine righteous persons who do not need to repent. God was in sorrow at the wickedness that mankind had gotten into, so whenever a single person wants to change and get right with God, God is happy. When our hearts respond to the Father Love sacrifice, God is happy that His plan of redemption for mankind has not been in vain. Jesus Christ, the Son of God, rejoices. Jesus' whole earthly life was spent in making the way for mankind to be forgiven and made right with God, the Father.

Every time a person repents (changes their mind) and turns to Him for salvation, Jesus overflows with joy that His willingness to lay down His life was worth it. The Holy Spirit rejoices. The Angels rejoice. Throughout the history of mankind, angels have been sent by God to help prophets preach and show mankind God's plan. The angels were privileged to make the announcement that the Messiah had been born in the little town of Bethlehem:

That night there were shepherds staying in the fields nearby, guarding their flocks of
sheep. Suddenly, an angel of the Lord appeared among them, and the radiance of
the Lord's glory surrounded them. They were terrified, but the angel reassured them.
"Don't be afraid!" he said. "I bring you good news that will bring great joy to all

people. The Savior—yes, the Messiah, the Lord—has been born today in Bethlehem, the city of David! And you will recognize him by this sign: You will find a baby wrapped snugly in strips of cloth, lying in a manger." Suddenly, the angel was joined by a vast host of others—the armies of heaven—praising God and saying, "Glory to God in highest heaven, and peace on earth to those with whom God is pleased." When the angels had returned to heaven, the shepherds said to each other, "Let's go to Bethlehem! Let's see this thing that has happened, which the Lord has told us about." (Luke 2:8–15 NLT)

The role of angels in God's plan is revealed in Hebrews (1:14 ASV): "Are they not all ministering spirits, sent forth to do service for the sake of them that shall inherit salvation?" Angels are sent forth to protect us from the adversary and lead us home to the Father's embrace.

If you have not invited Jesus to be Lord of your life, or if you're struggling with addiction, depression, suicide, homosexuality, or condemnation, I want you to know that God loves you. You are not reading this book by accident. God is reaching out to you to believe and trust Him. He loves you so much. Most people view homosexuality and addiction as a stronger bondage and more difficult sin from which to break free, but not God. God sees all the pain. He sees the feelings of rejection, shame, loneliness, and condemnation. God sees the behavior and chooses to love and rescue. He sees his children broken. Yes, God sees us from the inside out. It's only the love of God that can heal and restore us to wholeness. Once we allow God to love us, we can embrace our identity as his beloved child.

The Bible is the very breath of God and is a completely reliable source for determining a person's belief as well as instructing them in righteousness. The writer of Proverbs says, "Every way of a man is right in his own eyes, But the LORD weighs the hearts" (21:2–3 NKJV).

As we determine how homosexuality weighs on the scale of God's righteousness, a biblical perspective is in order. We are all shaped by our experiences in life. We do not choose to be born. We do not choose our parents. We do not choose the country of our birth or the immediate circumstances of our upbringing. Whether the abuse is derogatory, verbal, sexual, physical, or mental maltreatment, the heart of man gets wounded. When the soul of a man is wounded, the immediate response is to fill the pain with a form of love. Emotional pain is like an infection. If healing ointment isn't applied to the wound, any mention or attention to it brings pain.

The truth is, none of us want to feel insecure and lonely. Perhaps, like me, you are tired and desiring peace. In order for our hearts to heal, we need the right healing ointment. God the father wants to take your hand and walk you through your pain. God will spend as much time and as many years as possible to help you through it. He loves you. He wants to gently apply the daily ointment of his Holy Spirit to your heart until your heart is healed. "He heals the brokenhearted and binds up their wounds" (Psalm 147:3 NKJV).

God calls us to trust His Son as our Savior, and, in doing so, He declares that we have a brand new identity and nature. You see, God gets it right side up. He declares what we are, and then our actions begin to conform to that identity. He extends the gift of no condemnation, which empowers us to have the victory over sin. God knows that what we believe about ourselves, ultimately, will influence our behavior. He knows that how we see ourselves has power over how we live. He knows that when we see ourselves the way He sees us, it will change our lives. And He declares every Christian to have a brand new identity, an identity, which is so revolutionary in its meaning, that it will change not only our lives, but also the world.

God does not love us because we are valuable; rather we are valuable because God loves us. God's love is constant, never changing. So is our worth. The truth is that we are children of God, and that means that we are valued, loved, cared for, and significant.

There's no perfect prayer; it's simply, "God help me, I need you. I am sorry, and I repent. I ask you to forgive me. I believe that you died on the cross for me, to save me. You did what I could not do for myself. I come to you now and ask you to take control of my life; I give it to you. Help me to live every day in complete trust of your love for me. I love you, Lord, and I thank you for sending your Holy Spirit to live in me to teach me and reveal your love for me. I thank you, Lord; I will spend all eternity with you. Amen."

When you pray this, Christ Jesus will come and be with you forever, promising to never leave or forsake you. He will walk with you and help you face the dark painful areas of your life that have been shattered. I understand that wounds have been cut deeply. But the pain must be honestly acknowledged, brought to the surface, and released into His hands in order for the wounds to be healed. You matter to God. He wants to help you and to heal you. He wants to cancel every word spoken over your life that has caused pain, and He wants to speak His word of love and truth into your heart. He loves you!

CHAPTER 18

Prodigal Prayer

FATHER GOD, I come in Jesus' name in behalf of _____.
I stand in agreement to your Word (Ezekiel 34) that by your grace and
mercy _____ will receive healing and restoration to
his or her life. Father, I thank you that angels have been sent to minister to
_____. I set myself in agreement with Your Word, and I
thank you for the redemptive power of the cross.

Father, I ask in Jesus name to open the eyes of _____.
I thank you, Father, that the chains of condemnation will be loose and
_____ will come out of the snare of the devil and
make Jesus, Lord. Father, I thank you for the blood of Jesus, which has been
spoken in behalf of _____. Nothing is more pow-
erful than the blood of Your Son, Jesus. I thank you, Father for bringing
_____ back home.

I also tell you this: If two of you on agree here on earth concerning anything you ask, my
Father in heaven will do it for you. (Matthew 18:19 NLT)

For this is what t*he Sovereign Lord says: I myself will search and find my sheep. I will*
be like a shepherd looking for his scattered flock. I will find my sheep and rescue them from all
the places where they were scattered on that dark and cloudy day. I myself will tend my sheep
and give them a place to lie down in peace, says the Sovereign LORD. I will search for my lost
ones who strayed away, and I will bring them safely home again. I will bandage the injured
and strengthen the weak. But I will destroy those who are fat and powerful. I will feed them,
yes—feed them justice" (Ezekiel 34:11–12; 15–16 NLT)

Acknowledgements

First and foremost, I would like to thank my Father God for giving me the strength and fortitude it took to complete this project. I would like to express my gratitude to the many people who saw me through this book: those who provided support, talked things over, read, wrote, offered comments, assisted in the editing, proofreading, and design. I would like to thank Teri Gambill and Virginia Chatham for helping me in the editorial process.

For my parents:

Above all, I want to thank my parents, who supported and encouraged me. "Mom, I want to thank you for your persistent prayers and for never giving up on me. You never condemned me but extended love and grace." "Dad, I want to thank you for your humility. You have shown me that strength lies in surrender. Thank you for turning to God for our family's restorations. You have shown me an example of how a man should treat his wife and family by placing us in the hands of God. I have watched your faithful love and care for mom; it has opened my heart to welcome God's design—a godly man that will love and honor me like you love mom."

For my sisters:

Thank you for always keeping an open door and listening ear. Thank you for never speaking words of condemnation or excluding me from family gatherings. Thank you for your consistent prayers and love.

For Shannon and Randy Stevenson, Jordan Mercedes Berry, Robin Ellison:

Thank you for your friendship. The Lord has used you to encourage me to step out and begin walking out the dreams he's placed in my heart. You were the first to see the gifts and calling the Lord's placed in me and began calling them forth. Thank you for your words of wisdom to face and slay my giant of fear. I could not have asked for better partners in ministry.

Stay Connected with Amy

Connect with Amy through these social media channels.

Thejourneyoneway.blogspot.com

Facebook.com.\amy.l.kemp.3

Prayer request

If you have a prayer request, you can share it with our online community for support at facebook.com\amy.l.kemp.3 or submit a request to amyleekemp@gmail.com

Healing is a process that begins with prayer and faith. I believe in the power of prayer. I will stand with you and believe with you for God to move in your behalf.

Jeremiah 33:3 "Call to Me, and **I will** answer **you**..."

I would like to hear from you

If you have prayed the salvation prayer or if you have a testimony to share after reading this book, please send me an email at amyleekemp@gmail.com

Author Bio

Amy Lee Kemp has served God for the past 5 years with ministries throughout the United States and Europe. Amy Lee Kemp, a single woman, sister of three, aunt to 5 nieces and 3 nephews, and great aunt to 3 beautiful girls, is a resident of Tyler, Texas, where Prodigal Daughter Ministries is based. She is a speaker and author whose message of hope has changed the lives of many believers and unbelievers alike. Her passion is teaching and preaching the Word of God with an emphasis on overcoming hardships, living in victory, and understanding the authority that is available to every Christian through the sacrifice of Jesus Christ.

From hopeless to hopeful, Amy Lee Kemp shares her triumphant story with a society that is bombarded with story after story of defeat, destruction and brokenness. A refreshing promise of hope is renewed in people everywhere as they listen to the account of a young woman's despair growing into a flourishing and rewarding life of forgiveness, love and victory. She believes that God has given her a special grace to be able to make it through these trials and recover so that she could help others to do the same.

Amy desires to use her gifts and experiences to stamp out the darkness of deception and bring forth the light of Jesus Christ so that all may know the truth, love and peace that are free for them to receive.

Amy's testimony has been featured in a national Christian magazine "Domino Magazine", national newspaper, and the television program, The 700 Club.

Amy Lee Kemp is a dynamic motivational speaker and teacher who is intensely biblical, extremely passionate and practical. As a Sunday speaker, a woman's conference, youth conference, retreat speaker, or through her writing, Amy stands for truth and inspires others to grow in their knowledge of the benefits of being a child of God. Amy desires to walk hand in hand with others through her speaking and lead them into the loving embrace of Jesus.

Speaking Topics:
Women's Ministry
Youth / Teen
Victorious Living

Partner with Me Today

I'M INVITING YOU to partner with me. This way the full impact of bringing the light of Christ to many. This means that you not only contribute financially, but you are a part of bringing freedom and light to others. The gospel is free but the means to get the gospel to the lost cost. I pray you consider partnering with me today.

Our Ministry is to Love people, God will Heal them!

Together, we'll make a difference...

Faith brings vision and it also changes culture! Together we will impact lives with the love and light of Jesus Christ. Together we will reach young boys and girls who cut or are suicidal, those who struggle with identity issues, and the homeless and prostitutes. Together we will also reach those who know of God but no have never understood His love and gift of forgiveness. Together we will see God's love heal lives.

Thanks to the support of generous individual donors many have heard the Good News and received the gift of salvation. Your gifts make it possible for me to serve and love people. I welcome all levels of donation, whether it's a one-time gift or a monthly donation. Together the Kingdom of God is advance and Jesus is glorified.

When God is fighting for you, "**One** man can chase a thousand [Joshua 23:10] and **two** shall put ten thousand to flight."

http://thejourneyoneway.blogspot.com

Recommended Resources

Joseph Prince "Destined to Reign" and "Power of right believing"

Joyce Meyer "Battlefield of the Mind"

Sarah Young "Jesus Calling" Devotional

The Bible

"You didn't choose me, remember; I chose you…"
John 15:16 MSG

22403838R00055

Made in the USA
San Bernardino, CA
05 July 2015